Christ Is Supreme!

Discipleship Lessons from

Colossians and Philemon

A Bible Study Commentary for Personal Devotional Use, Small Groups or
Sunday School Classes, and Sermon Preparation for Pastors and Teachers

JesusWalk® Bible Study Series

by Dr. Ralph F. Wilson
Director, Joyful Heart Renewal Ministries

Additional books, and reprint licenses are available at:
www.jesuswalk.com/books/colossians.htm

Free Participant Guide handout sheets are available at:
www.jesuswalk.com/colossians/colossians-lesson-handouts.pdf

JesusWalk® Publications
Loomis, California

Paperback

ISBN-13: 978-0-9819721-7-6
ISBN-10: 098197217

Library of Congress Control Number: 2010905063

Library of Congress subject headings:
Bible. - N.T. – Colossians – Commentaries.
Bible. - N.T. - Philemon - Commentaries.

Suggested Classifications
Dewey Decimal System: 227.7
Library of Congress: BS2715.53

Published by JesusWalk® Publications, P.O. Box 565, Loomis, CA 95650-0565, USA.

JesusWalk is a registered trademark and Joyful Heart is a trademark of Joyful Heart
Renewal Ministries.

Unless otherwise noted, all the Bible verses quoted are from the New International
Version (International Bible Society, 1973, 1978), used by permission.

100412

Preface

To the immature, rule-keeping can feel more "religious" than a spiritual devotion to Christ himself.

That was the temptation the Colossian church was facing. Their pastor trekked one thousand miles to Rome from what is now Turkey to find Paul and ask him to write a letter that would lay out true Christianity for his church members, in order to protect them from false teachers intent on picking them off and persuading them to adopt another faith.

The letter that Paul wrote in response to Epaphras' plea has been preserved as Paul's Letter to the Colossians. Outward religion, is not the answer, says Paul. Christ is both supreme and sufficient – we need nothing beyond him to complete our faith.

The letter provides us with one of the most compelling visions in all the New Testament of who Jesus Christ actually is, in all his majesty and glory – the image of the invisible God, existing before all things, Creator of everything, Sustainer, Head, Beginning, First-to-Be-Resurrected – the fullness of God in bodily form. Christ is preeminent!

This nine-week Bible study of Colossians and Philemon both awes us in its revelation of Christ and anchors us in practical guidelines for Christian living.

I invite you to join me in a nine-week Bible study of Colossians and Philemon.

Dr. Ralph F. Wilson
Loomis, California
April 16, 2010

Reprint Guidelines

Copying the Handouts. In some cases, small groups or Sunday school classes would like to use these notes to study this material. That's great. An appendix provides copies of handouts designed for classes and small groups. There is no charge whatsoever to print out as many copies of the handouts as you need for participants.

All charts and notes are copyrighted and must bear the line: "Copyright © 2010, Ralph F. Wilson. All rights reserved. Reprinted by permission."

You may not resell these notes to other groups or individuals outside your congregation. You may, however, charge people in your group enough to cover your copying costs.

Copying the book (or the majority of it) in your congregation or group, you are requested to purchase a reprint license for each book. A Reprint License, $2.50 for each copy is available for purchase at

www.jesuswalk.com/books/colossians.htm

Or you may send a check to:

> Dr. Ralph F. Wilson
> JesusWalk Publications
> PO Box 565
> Loomis, CA 95650, USA

The Scripture says,

> "The laborer is worthy of his hire" (Luke 10:7) and "Anyone who receives instruction in the word must share all good things with his instructor" (Galatians 6:6).

However, if you are from a third world country or an area where it is difficult to transmit money, please make a small contribution instead to help the poor in your community.

Online Bible Study Forum

Each chapter in this study contains four or five questions to help you learn and process what you've been studying. As you engage your mind in the attempt to frame an answer, you'll begin to understand the issues raised in the Scripture text and the implications of applying the principles in your own life.

But learning is better with others. This book began as an interactive e-mail Bible study. One component of this learning approach has been to give students a chance to post their answers to the questions in an online Forum and read how others answered the questions as a way of deepening learning. You'll find that each of the questions in the chapters contains a web address where you, too, can take advantage of the Forum.

However, if you want to participate in the Forum, you'll need to agree to some basic guidelines (www.jesuswalk.com/admin/pu_forum_guidelines.htm). In short:

- No denomination or religion bashing.
- Practice a loving spirit.
- Comments may be removed in the future.
- Stay on topic.
- Be discrete. Don't give out your e-mail address or share things too personal.

If you haven't participated in the Forum before, you'll need to register first. To keep from getting confused, why don't you Read the Instructions for the Forum. They will explain exactly how to register (www.joyfulheart.com/forums/instructions.htm).

Once you've registered for the Forum you can introduce yourself to others in this study (www.joyfulheart.com/forums/index.php?showtopic=955) and get started with the questions posed in each chapter.

Table of Contents

References and Abbreviations

While most of the commentaries include two or more other Pauline epistles, in the footnotes I'll be referring to the appropriate commentaries only with the term "Colossians."

BDAG	Walter Bauer and Frederick William Danker, A Greek-English Lexicon of the New Testament and Other Early Christian Literature (Third Edition; based on previous English editions by W.F. Arndt, F.W. Gingrich, and F.W. Danker; University of Chicago Press, 1957, 1979, 2000). ISBN 0226039331.
Bruce	F.F. Bruce, The Epistles to the Colossians, to Philemon, and to the Ephesians (New International Commentary on the New Testament; Eerdmans, 1984).
DPL	Gerald F. Hawthorne, Ralph P. Martin, and Daniel Reid (editors), Dictionary of Paul and His Letters (InterVarsity Press, 1993). ISBN 0830817786.
ISBE	Geoffrey W. Bromiley (general editor), The International Standard Bible Encyclopedia (Eerdmans, 1979-1988; fully revised from the 1915 edition). ISBN: 0802837859.
KJV	King James Version (Authorized Version, 1611).
Lightfoot	J.B. Lightfoot, *Saint Paul's Epistles to the Colossians and to Philemon* (Zondervan, 1959; reprinted from Macmillan and Company, revised 1879 edition).
Moo	Douglas J. Moo, The Letters to the Colossians and to Philemon (Pillar New Testament Commentary; Eerdmans, 2008). ISBN 0802837271.
NIV	New International Version (International Bible Society, 1973, 1978).
NRSV	New Revised Standard Version (Division of Christian Education of the National Council of Churches of Christ USA, 1989).
Robertson	A.T. Robertson, Word Pictures in the New Testament (Broadman Press, 1930, 6 volumes). Used in an electronic version.
TDNT	Theological Dictionary of the New Testament, Gerhard Kittel and

Gerhard Friedrich (editors), Geoffrey W. Bromiley (translator and editor), (Eerdmans, 1964-1976; translated from Theologisches Wörterbuch zum Neuen Testament, ten volume edition). CD-ROM, ISBN 1577990994.

Thayer   Joseph Henry Thayer, Greek-English Lexicon of the New Testament (Associated Publishers and Authors, n.d., reprinted from 1889 edition). Used in an electronic version. ISBN 1565632095.

Vincent   Marvin R. Vincent, Vincent's Word Studies in the New Testament (1886; reprinted: Hendrickson, 1985). ISBN 0917006305. Used in an electronic version.

Wright   N.T. Wright, Colossians and Philemon (Tyndale New Testament Commentaries; IVP Academic, 1986). ISBN 083084242X.

Introduction to Colossians

The City of Colossae

Colossae or Colosse was an ancient city in the Lycus River valley, about 100 miles east of the great, cosmopolitan capital city of Ephesus, located in the Roman province of Asia, in present-day Turkey.

Colossae was the smallest of three cities in the Lycus Valley – along with Laodicea (12 miles west) and Hierapolis (15 miles northwest). Each of these cities had Christian churches (4:13-16).

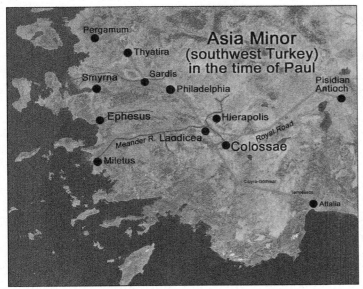

Though these cities were far from the big city, they weren't isolated, since they were situated near the great Persian Royal Road that ran from Ephesus and Sardis in the West to the Euphrates and on to Persia in the East.[1]

At one point in the fourth or third centuries BC, Colossae had been the most important of the three cities, known for its flourishing textile industry and high-quality dark red wool, known as "Colossian wool." But after the north-south road was moved west to pass through Laodicea, Colossae began to decline.

Roman historian Tacitus mentions an earthquake that destroyed Laodicea in 60-61 AD.[2] Laodicea was rebuilt quickly. We don't know how long it took to rebuild Colossae. Today, however, nothing remains of Colossae above ground. The tell (acropolis or

---

[1] The best source for information on the Royal Road is David French, "Pre- and Early-Roman Roads of Asia Minor. The Persian Royal Road," *Iran*, Vol. 36 (1998), pp. 15-43 (British Institute of Persian Studies).

[2] Tacitus, Annals 14.27. This is probably the same earthquake that destroyed Laodicea, Hierapolis, and Colosse in 64 AD, mentioned by Eusebius (*Chronicle* 1.21-22).

mound) of the city has not been excavated, though the contour of an outdoor amphitheater is discernable on the site.

The Peoples of Colossae

The population of Colossae was probably quite diverse – especially in light of the nearby highway.

We know that Antiochus III had settled about 2,000 Jewish families in the general area in 213 BC.[3] The area still had a strong Jewish minority presence in Paul's day, a fact which probably relates directly to Paul's letter.

Proximity to the nearby highways ensured that the Colossians were

The tell or acropolis of the city has not been excavated. It appears darkened because the vegetation had been burned off recently. Photo copyright by HolyLandPhotos.org. Used by permission.

exposed to the latest ideas, which then mixed together with other ideas. Thus the Christian church was subject to syncretism with other religious movements.

Colossians is apparently written primarily to Gentile Christians. We observe:

- Paul's description of their conversion in terms more appropriate to Gentiles, rather than to Jews (1:12, 21)

- He mentions the mystery revealed "among the Gentiles" (1:27)

- The sins mentioned are more typical of Gentiles, than of Jews (3:5)

---

[3] Josephus, Antiquities of the Jews, 12.3.4. As a way to quell a rebellion in Phrygia and Lydia, Antiochus III ordered that Jewish families be relocated from Babylon (where they had been exiled in the sixth century BC) to the area of Phrygia, in the general area where Colossae is located. They were permitted to observe their own laws, given land, and exempted from taxation for 10 years.

- He includes neither Old Testament quotations nor any explicit reference to the law.[4]

Though he writes primarily to Gentile Christians, the heresy that Paul was fighting seems to have Jewish roots, as is discussed below.

History of the Church

While Paul had probably passed through Colossae on his second missionary journey, he didn't found the church at Colossae – directly. Rather, it was founded by Epaphras, whom Paul mentions in this letter (1:7-8; 4:12-13).

Paul had been preaching in the "big city" of Ephesus, about 100 miles west of Colossae from 53 to 55 AD. His ministry was quite effective, first in the synagogue and later in the rented lecture hall of Tyrannus.

"This went on for two years, so that all the Jews and Greeks who lived in the province of Asia heard the word of the Lord." (Acts 19:10)

Paul didn't travel through the province of Asia, but people came to him to learn about Jesus, and then took the message of the gospel to their own hometowns. Epaphras was undoubtedly one of these.

Occasion of the Letter

Paul is in prison "for the sake of the gospel" (4:3, 10), probably in Rome. Epaphras, the pastor of the Colossian church, has come to Paul's place of imprisonment. In his letter to Philemon, Paul speaks of Epaphras as "my fellow prisoner in Christ Jesus" (Philemon 1:23).

No doubt, Epaphras has come to consult with Paul about the heresy that was causing problems in the Colossian church. So Paul writes a letter to the Colossians designed to expose and stop the heresy and to encourage the church in their new Christian faith. Since Epaphras can't return at this time, Paul sends the letter by the hand of his co-worker Tychicus (4:7-8).

Authorship

From earliest times through the mid-1800s, the Letter to the Colossians has been accepted at face value as from "Paul, an apostle of Christ Jesus" (1:1). Colossians is

---

[4] Moo, *Colossians*, pp. 28-29.

alluded to by Clement of Rome (97-98 AD),[5] Ignatius (about 110 AD),[6] and the Letter of Barnabas (182-188 AD),[7] was included in Marcion's canon (c. 144 AD) and the Muratorian Canon (c. 190-217 AD), and was quoted by Irenaeus (c. 180),[8] Theophilus of Antioch (176-186 AD),[9] Clement of Alexandria (c. 193-220),[10] Tertullian (198-220 AD),[11] Origen (225-254),[12] and Eusebius. Colossians is firmly established in the canon of the Christian church.

However, in recent years it has become widely popular to question Pauline authorship of Colossians (as well as Ephesians and Philippians) on the grounds of style and a more advanced theology than Paul's "accepted" letters.

So far as style goes, the vocabulary of Colossians includes a number of words not found elsewhere in Paul's letters. But that can be explained by Paul's two-fold role as both "an apologist for Christianity to the intellectual world of paganism," as well as defending the gospel within the church. F.F. Bruce comments:

> "As apologist to the Gentiles, he may have been the first to meet his pagan opponents on their own ground and use their language in a Christian sense, in order to show that the problems to which they unsuccessfully sought an answer elsewhere found their solution in the gospel."[13]

While Colossians bears differences from other Pauline epistles, it includes the Pauline touch through and through. The arguments positing a different author than Paul are extremely speculative and, frankly, create more problems than they purport to solve. I believe that an excellent case can be made that Colossians was written by the Apostle Paul himself.

Place and Date of Origin

If Paul is the author, as I believe, the question remains: During which of his prison periods was the letter written? Various scholars have argued for his writing it during

---

[5] Clement of Rome, *1 Clement* 24:1 (Col 1:18).
[6] Ignatius, *To the Ephesians* c. iii uses the wording of Colossians 1:23.
[7] *Letter of Barnabas* 12. (Col. 1:16).
[8] Irenaeus, *Against Heresies* 3.14.1.
[9] Theophilus of Antioch (176-186 AD), *Ad Autolycum* (Col 1:15).
[10] Clement of Alexandria, *Stromata* 5.12 (Col 2:2b-3).
[11] Tertullian, *De Praescriptione*, c. 7; *On the Resurrection of the Flesh*, 23 (Col. 1:21).
[12] Origen of Alexandria, *De Principiis* 1.5 (Col. 1:15).
[13] Bruce, *Colossians*, p. 29, citing H. Chadwick, "All Things to All Men," p. 272.

imprisonments at Ephesus (c. 52-55 AD),[14] Caesarea (c. 57-59 AD), and Rome (c. 60-62 AD). Arguments for one place or another are based on the best fit of circumstances, companions present, visitors during imprisonment, the nature of the false teaching combated, the state of advance of Pauline theology, and an earthquake in 60-61 AD that devastated Colossae.

However, most scholars who accept Pauline authorship date the Letter to the Colossians during Paul's first imprisonment in Rome, approximately 60-62 AD (Acts 20:31-32). That makes the most sense to me.

The Lycus Valley. Photo copyright by HolyLandPhotos.org. Used by permission.

The Nature of the "Colossian Heresy"

The particular heresy that Paul addresses in Colossae is difficult to pin down exactly. It has similarities – and differences – with doctrinal problems that Paul addresses in other churches.

Just what is the "Colossian heresy"? As we read between the lines in 2:8-25 we can begin to discern its shape. The heresy seems to have had these elements:

---

[14] Wright (*Colossians*, pp. 37-42) argues for an Ephesian location around in the early 50s AD. While possible, an Ephesian imprisonment is only hinted at in Scripture (1 Corinthians 15:32; 2 Corinthians 1:8), so I doubt that it was long enough to compose Colossians and the other "prison epistles."

1. **A belief system**, called a "hollow and deceptive philosophy" (2:8).

2. **Tradition-based**, "depends on human tradition" (2:8, 22).

3. **Elemental spiritual forces** underlie the system (2:8).

4. **Not Christ-centered**, the teaching doesn't "depend on ... Christ" (2:8).

5. **Food restrictions and Jewish "holy days"** are involved (2:16).

6. **Ascetic disciplines** are encouraged (2:18, 23).

7. **Angel worship** is central (2:18).

8. **Visionary experiences** are touted (2:18).

9. **Pride** characterizes the proponents (2:18).

10. **Losing connection with Christ** is the result (2:19).

11. **Rule-keeping** is urged (2:20-23).

Most scholars agree on these points. Three more possible points are less certain.

12. **"Fullness" language** (1:19; 2:9, 10) suggests that a "fullness" of spiritual experience couldn't be found in Christ alone. The vocabulary is found in both Gnosticism and Stoicism.

13. **Circumcision** is advocated (2:11, 13; 3:11) – perhaps.

14. **Christ is being denigrated** – perhaps – though this may reflect Paul's cure more than the active teaching of his opponents. [15]

Who Are the False Teachers?

The identity of the false teachers at Colossae has been widely debated. The major views tend to cluster around four explanations:

1. **Mystery religions** have been argued by some as one of the sources of the heresy, but this is hard to pin down or prove.

2. **Gnosticism** would assume a much later composition of this letter, since full-blown Gnosticism didn't mature until the mid-second century AD. It is possible, however, to see some incipient Gnostic elements in the false teachers' position. [16]

---

[15] Listed by Moo, *Colossians*, pp. 50-51.

3. **Jewish mysticism** was one of the strands of Judaism that was flourishing at the time. Bruce argues for a background of Jewish *merkabah* mysticism, which gave way to exercises designed to facilitate entry into the vision of the heavenly chariot (Hebrew *merkābâ*, of Ezekiel's vision of the wheel within the wheel, Ezekiel 1:15-26).[17] Wright sees Colossians as a warning against Judaism itself.[18]

4. **A mixture of teachings** is most likely, I think. We would like to see a simple opponent, but movements are inevitably affected by the winds of thought swirling through the culture. Clinton Arnold argues for a syncretism or combination of Phrygian[19] folk belief, local folk Judaism, and Christianity.[20]

We just don't have enough information to determine the exact identity of the Colossian heretics beyond the basic outlines. However, these teachers seem to represent an ascetic and mystical form of Jewish piety mixed with local folk belief, perhaps with Christian overtones, since Paul says that they weren't "holding fast to the Head" (2:19).

Whoever they were, Paul's prescription is a focus on the sufficiency and supremacy of Christ as the antidote to being pulled away to a heresy that promised greater "fullness."

Purpose of the Letter

Colossians seems to have been written with two purposes in mind:

1. To encourage and ground this relatively new Christian community, and

2. To protect them from the seduction of false teachers, probably from a variety of mystical Judaism, that tended to denigrate these Gentile Christians' faith in Christ in favor of the claims of Judaism.

As you study Colossians, I'm sure you'll not only be blessed with a greater knowledge of Christ, you'll also get some practical handles on living a life consistent with his teaching and values.

---

[16] Ralph P. Martin, *Colossians and Philemon* (New Century Bible; London: Oliphants, 1974), pp. 8-19 interprets the heresy in mainly Gnostic terms. But he doesn't demonstrate adequately that these later Gnostic elements were present in Asia Minor at the time Colossians was written.

[17] Bruce, *Colossians*, pp. 19-26.

[18] Wright, *Colossians*, pp. 26-33.

[19] Phrygia is the name of the region in which Colossae is located.

[20] Arnold's position is endorsed by Moo, *Colossians*, pp. 57-59.

1. A Prayer for the Colossian Believers (Colossians 1:1-14)

As Paul begins this letter, in the first few verses he introduces himself, explains the world-wide scope of the Christian movement, and then tells the Colossians how he is praying for them. These prayers, especially, give us a window into the Apostle's heart, and help us understand what Christian discipleship is really all about.

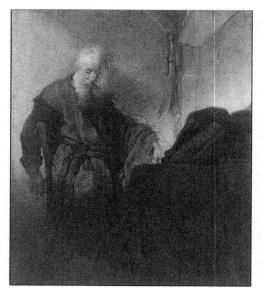

The Situation

Though Paul had never seen the Colossian church in person, you can sense his love for them in the first few verses of this letter.

It's likely that Paul had passed by Colossae on his way to the "big city" of Ephesus, but he had never been to the church in Colossae. In fact, it hadn't existed when he had gone past it on the great Royal Highway from the East that ended in Sardis and Ephesus, 100 miles west.

Rembrandt, "St Paul at his Writing-Desk" (1629), oil on wood, 47.2 x 38 cm., Germanisches Nationalmuseum, Nuremberg.

Paul spent nearly three years in Ephesus, preaching first in the synagogue, then later, when he had been kicked out, he rented the lecture hall of Tyrannus, where he taught the new disciples.

Epaphras was one of these new disciples. No doubt, while in Ephesus, he heard of Paul, sat under his teaching, and became a Christian. Then he went back to Colossae and started a church (1:7-8). Now Epaphras has come to Rome, sought Paul out, and has asked him to write a letter to encourage and help stabilize the Colossian believers in the face of false teaching.

Paul and Timothy, the Senders (1:1)

And so Paul begins the letter.

"[1] Paul, an apostle of Christ Jesus by the will[1] of God, and Timothy our brother, [2] To the holy and faithful brothers in Christ at Colosse: Grace and peace to you from God our Father." (1:1-2)

Greek letters in Paul's time began with a kind of formula: first the name of the sender, then the name of the recipient, and finally a greeting.

Paul introduces himself in a kind of formal manner:

"Paul an apostle of Christ Jesus by the will of God." (1:1a)

This is for two reasons. First, the Colossians have never met Paul. Second, he needs to establish his authority so that he can teach them and warn them of the heresy that threatens the church. Apostle, means, "one sent on a commission." He is not self-appointed. He is an apostle "by the will of God." He is commissioned by God himself and speaks with God's authority.

Notice the inverse word order of "Christ Jesus," different than what we're used to. Paul's reason is to emphasize Jesus' messiahship. Christ, of course, means, "messiah," so this reads: Messiah Jesus. As we'll see as the letter unfolds, one of the threats is from a Jewish group that may be questioning Jesus' messiahship and prominence. So Paul begins with Christ's awesome title from the very first sentence.

To the Colossian Believers (1:2)

"To the holy and faithful brothers in Christ at Colosse: Grace and peace to you from God our Father." (1:2)

He addresses the Colossian believers as "holy and faithful." "Holy," in that they are set apart to God, they are not their own. [2] And "faithful," in that they are both full of faith and are acting in a faithful and trustworthy manner (the word can have both connotations).[3]

Now Paul offers them a greeting:

"Grace and peace to you from God our Father." (1:2)

---

[1] *Thelēma*, "the act of willing or desiring, subjective sense, will" (BDAG 447, 2b).

[2] *Hagios*, originally a cultic concept, of the quality possessed by things and persons that could approach a divinity, here, "believers, loyal followers, saints, of Christians as consecrated to God" (BDAG 11, 2dβ).

[3] *Pistos*, can mean either worthy of trust, belief, or, as here, "pertaining to being trusting, trusting, cherishing faith/trust" (BDAG 823, 2).

"Grace" was the characteristic Greek greeting, which extended a word of favor (or grace) to the person greeted. "Peace" (*shalom* in Hebrew) was the characteristic Jewish greeting. Paul combines these greetings and then identifies the source of the blessings: "God our Father."

Thanksgiving for the Colossians' Faith and Love (1:3-6)

Now Paul lets his readers know of his personal concern for them and his joy in their faith:

> "We always thank God, the Father of our Lord Jesus Christ, when we pray for you." (1:3)

Though Paul has not seen their face, he prays for this new Colossian church. "Pray" is in the present tense, suggesting continuing, ongoing action. Paul was in the habit of praying for the Colossians. And whenever he prays, he gives thanks. Why? Because he has heard good things about this church – both by reputation and from the reports brought by Epaphras.

> "We thank God ... ⁴ because we have heard of your faith in Christ Jesus and of the love you have for all the saints – ⁵ the faith and love that spring from the hope that is stored up for you in heaven and that you have already heard about in the word of truth, the gospel ⁶ that has come to you." (1:4-6a)

It's a complicated sentence – but get used to it. Sometimes in Greek, Paul can go on for a whole paragraph or two without a period. Mercifully, our English translations smooth out these run-on sentences a bit.

Here are three causes for Paul's thanksgiving:

1. **Faith in Christ Jesus**. They believe in Messiah Jesus.

2. **Love for the all the saints**. This church has an especially open and far-reaching love. Instead of only loving people who are "just like them," they have demonstrated a love for "saints" (people set apart to God) from a variety of places, who have probably stopped in Colossae to rest. And when they arrived they were shown generous hospitality and showered with love.

Faith, that is, belief in Jesus, can be faked. Love can be put on – at least for a while. But faith and love together are quintessential earmarks of solid Christians. Notice the third cause, from which the first two spring: [4]

3. **Hope** "that is stored up for you in heaven" (1:5). Their focus is not this-worldly, but other-worldly, set upon an inheritance "stored up" for them in heaven. This word "stored up" (NIV), "laid up" (NRSV, KJV) is *apokeimai*, originally, "to put away for safekeeping," here, "to reserve as award or recompense, reserve," a common term in honorary documents expressing appreciation for sense of civic or other communal responsibility.[5]

Here we have the three virtues that Paul talked about at the end of the "Love Chapter," 1 Corinthians 13.

"And now these three remain: faith, hope and love. But the greatest of these is love." (1 Corinthians 13:13)

You've already heard about this hope, Paul says, "... in the word of truth, the gospel that has come to you" (1:5b).

The Gospel is Multiplying (1:5b-6)

The Colossians have been enticed by the false teachers to turn from Christ to a faith where he wasn't at the center. So Paul explains that they are not just an isolated few, but part of a world-wide movement.

"All over the world this gospel is bearing fruit and growing, just as it has been doing among you since the day you heard it and understood God's grace in all its truth." (1:6)

The word "gospel" means "good news." Here it refers to the message of salvation in Jesus Christ. The gospel is active ("bearing fruit and growing"). It recalls the description

---

[4] The NIV adds a few words at the beginning of verse 5 to bring out the meaning of the preposition *dia*: "the faith and hope that spring from." Other translations are more brief: "because of" the hope (NRSV), "for" the hope (KJV). *Dia*, "through," here, is probably, a "marker of instrumentality or circumstance whereby something is accomplished or effected, by, via, through" -- probably as the "efficient cause," as expressed in the NRSV (BDAG 224, 3d).

[5] *Apokeimai*, BDAG 113, 2. Paul uses the word just before his death: "there is reserved for me the crown of righteousness" (2 Timothy 4:8, NRSV). Another use of this idea is to "store up for yourselves treasures in heaven" (Matthew 6:20), using the word *thēsaurizō* (from which we get our word "thesaurus"), to keep some material thing safe by storing it, lay up, store up, gather, save," then figuratively, "to do something that will bring about a future event or condition, store up" (BDAG 456, 2a).

of the word of God which is "living and active," which penetrates and judges (Hebrews 4:12).

Notice how Paul characterizes the gospel, with almost human characteristics:

- **Gospel** – "good news"

- **The word of truth**, that is a message that can be trusted. Dear friend, the gospel of Jesus' salvation is true. You can rely upon it.

- **Bearing fruit.**[6] What kind of fruit tree is the gospel? One that produces holy, transformed, born-anew Christians, believers in Jesus, who model their lives after Jesus' life.

- **Growing** (NIV, NRSV) is *auxanō*, "to become greater, grow, increase."[7] The early church had not stagnated or plateaued after a few years. The Christian movement was growing rapidly all over the known world. In the lifetime of the apostles the gospel reached Iraq and India under the Apostle Thomas, and perhaps Spain through the Apostle Paul. Their disciples then carried the good news to Europe and the British Isles, that were then Roman colonies and outposts. "Bearing fruit and growing" echo Jesus' Parable of the Sower where the seed ("the Word of God") in the good soil "produced a crop – a hundred, sixty or thirty times what was sown" (Matthew 13:8).

Where you live, it may not seem like the Christian movement is growing. In fact, in Western Europe and America, it seems to be contracting at present. But world-wide, the Christian movement is growing rapidly. Sub-Saharan Africa became predominately Christian by the end of the twentieth century, as did Korea. The Christian church is growing rapidly in China and South America, in parts of India, and elsewhere.

---

[6] "Bearing fruit" (NIV, NRSV), "bringeth forth fruit" (KJV) is *karpophoreō*, "to cause production of fruit or seeds, bear fruit/crops," here and in 1:10 used figuratively (BDAG 510, 2).
[7] *Auxanō*, BDAG 153, 2a. This word is omitted in the KJV, following K and a number of other later texts.

Q1. (Colossians 1:5-6) Paul glorifies the gospel, the good news. What words does he use to describe the action of the gospel in verses 5 and 6? Given the temptation the recipients have to adopt another religious philosophy, why do you think he reminds them of the world scope of the gospel's influence? What happens in our day when a church becomes embarrassed or unimpressed with the gospel message? How does this affect the church? http://www.joyfulheart.com/forums/index.php?showtopic=956

God's Grace (1:6b)

> "All over the world this gospel is bearing fruit and growing, just as it has been doing among you since the day you heard it and understood[8] God's grace in all its truth." (1:6)

Notice the key role of both hearing the gospel and understanding it. It is possible, of course, to hear the story of Jesus without understanding its implications. But when a person grasps "God's grace in all its truth," they turn to Jesus.

How many of your friends have heard the gospel, but not grasped the glorious truths of God's grace. "Grace" (*charis*) describes the nature of our salvation. Most people believe that they must work for their salvation. The wonderful truth of God's grace is that salvation is a free gift, granted by God, through Jesus Christ. All we do is to believe it – that is, embrace the truth for ourselves. The classic scripture on grace in the New Testament is:

> "For it is by grace you have been saved, through faith – and this not from yourselves, it is the gift of God – not by works, so that no one can boast." (Ephesians 2:8-9)

---

[8] "Understood" (NIV), "comprehended" (NRSV), "knew" (KJV) is *epiginōskō*, "to have knowledge of something or someone, know." Sometimes the preposition *epi-*, "upon" is felt in the meaning of the word, as here, "know exactly, completely, through and through" (BDAG 369, 1a). In compound words, *epi-* can intensify the word it modifies. In *epiginōskō*, "epi denotes mental direction toward, application to, that which is known" (Thayer on *epiginōskō*).

Epaphras, the Faithful Minister (1:7-8)

Now Paul mentions Epaphras, whom we assume is the founder of the church in Colossae:

> "7 You learned it from Epaphras, our dear fellow servant, who is a faithful minister of Christ on our behalf, 8 and who also told us of your love in the Spirit." (1:7-8)

See what it says about him:

- **"Dear"** (NIV, KJV), **"beloved"** (NRSV). Epaphras is dear not only to the Colossians, but also to Paul himself.

- **Fellow servant**. Paul acknowledges him as a colleague. And, as a mark of humility, refers to both Epaphras and himself as a "servant." The word is probably better translated, "fellow-slave," from the root *doulos*, "slave." This isn't about Paul and Epaphras, but about their Master, their Owner – Jesus! One of the first steps of Christian maturity is to realize that the Christian faith isn't about us – about our salvation and relief from some of our problems. It is about God and his Son Jesus. We are not the center, we are servants of the Central One.

- **Faithful**. "Faithful," of course, refers to Epaphras' reliability. He doesn't run hot and cold. He has proved himself trustworthy to carry out his responsibilities.

- **Minister of Christ**. This word is *diakonia*, "servant," especially as an "agent, intermediary, courier."[9] In America our high officials are called Secretary of State or President. But in Europe and much of the rest of the world, they are titled as Foreign Minister or Prime Minister. We represent Jesus in our little corner of the world. We are his personal emissaries to those we meet and live around.

Incidentally, the phrase "on our behalf" (NIV), "on your behalf" (NRSV), "for you" (KJV) is one of those instances where the Greek text isn't exactly clear, whether it should be "our" or "your." In this context "on your behalf" seems to make more sense to me. Epaphras has "told us of your love in the Spirit" (1:8).

While we're talking about Epaphras, let's look at the two other passages in the Bible where he is mentioned:

> "Epaphras, who is one of you and a servant of Christ Jesus, sends greetings. He is always wrestling in prayer for you, that you may stand firm in all the will of God, mature and fully assured." (4:12)

---

[9] *Diakonos*, BDAG 230, 1.

"Epaphras, my fellow prisoner in Christ Jesus, sends you greetings." (Philemon 23)

Epaphras was also a prisoner, who was either in jail with Paul or living with him under house arrest. We don't know the circumstances of Epaphras' imprisonment.

The other thing we learn about him is that he is a "prayer warrior." He wrestles in prayer for the Colossian believers – even from the distance of hundreds of miles that separate Rome (where we assume Paul was imprisoned) and Colossae.

Paul's Prayer for the Colossian Believers (1:9-12a)

"8b Epaphras ... who also told us of your love in the Spirit." (1:8b)

Epaphras has reported the love the Colossian believers have, prompted by the Holy Spirit within them. This expression of love – probably a profound love for God, but also an affection for Paul himself – prompts Paul to pray for them. And when he started praying for them, he never stopped.

"9 For this reason, since the day we heard about you, we have not stopped praying for you and asking God to fill you with the knowledge of his will through all spiritual wisdom and understanding. 10 And we pray this in order that you may live a life worthy of the Lord and may please him in every way: bearing fruit in every good work, growing in the knowledge of God, 11 being strengthened with all power according to his glorious might so that you may have great endurance and patience, and joyfully 12 giving thanks to the Father." (1:9-12a)

We're going to examine this prayer in some detail, since it instructs us both how to pray for other believers and what are the important pieces of the profile of a growing believer.

- To know God's will (1:9b).

- To have spiritual wisdom and understanding (1:9).

- To live a life worthy of Jesus, one that is pleasing to him (1:10a).

- To bear fruit by doing good works (1:10b).

- To grow in your knowledge of, or relationship to, God (1:10c).

- To be strengthened by God's power (1:11a) so that you have the qualities of endurance, patience, thankfulness, and joy (1:11b-12a).

So often we "dumb down" Christian discipleship to going to church, praying, and reading the Bible. But Paul describes discipleship in terms of qualities of life and ways of living. We have much to learn.

Knowing God (1:9-10)

The first element in the profile of a disciple is knowledge.

"... We have not stopped praying for you and asking God to fill you with the knowledge of his will through all spiritual wisdom and understanding" (1:9)

"... Growing in the knowledge of God" (1:10c)

When we approach the idea of "knowledge," we naturally think about absorbing facts and concepts. But in Scripture, knowledge often goes beyond this to knowing, being intimately acquainted with a person. As you recall, in Genesis, "Adam knew his wife" (Genesis 4:1) is a euphemism for "have sex with" – intimate relationship. God wants the disciples of Jesus to know him deeply – depth of relationship, not just theological reflection about God's nature.

In verse 9, Paul asks for "God to fill you with the knowledge of his will" – that is, an understanding of his purposes and way of doing things. In verse 10 he prays that they might be "... Growing in the knowledge of God" – that is, growing in relationship with him, getting better acquainted with the person of God.

Paul modifies the knowledge of God in verse 9 by saying, "through all spiritual wisdom and understanding."[10] Non-Christian philosophers (who Paul mentions in 2:8) may have wisdom and insight, but is speaking "spiritual" (*pneumatikos*) wisdom and knowledge, that is, given by the Spirit of God. Has the Holy Spirit made you wise and given you spiritual insight? That is Paul's prayer.

Bearing Fruit (1:10b)

Paul looks for results in one's life:

"... Bearing fruit in every good work...." (1:10b)

The fruit of this Spirit-given insight and wisdom is a life that pleases God. Paul describes this pleasing life as "worthy[11] of the Lord." This means both a life of worth

---

[10] *Synesis*, "the faculty of comprehension, intelligence, acuteness, shrewdness" (BDAG 970, 1b), perhaps, "insightfulness."

[11] *Axiōs*, "worthily, in a manner worthy of, suitably" (BDAG 94).

and a life that brings credit to the Lord. When Christians live sloppy, hypocritical, and unrighteous lives, we bring reproach on our Lord.

Are lives that are "unfruitful" really Christian? Two teachings come to mind – one from Paul, the other from James:

> "For we are God's workmanship, created in Christ Jesus to do good works, which God prepared in advance for us to do." (Ephesians 2:10)

> "What good is it, my brothers, if a man claims to have faith but has no deeds? Can such faith save him? ... Faith by itself, if it is not accompanied by action, is dead." (James 2:14, 17)

We are not saved by good works; we are saved for good works. If the fruit of good works is not in our lives – the fruit of the Spirit working in and through our lives – then how do we know we are true Christians?

Paul prays that the Colossians may be strengthened so they might have "great endurance and patience" (1:11) These are related words.

- **"Endure/endurance"** (NRSV, NIV), "patience" (KJV) is *hypomonē*, "the capacity to hold out or bear up in the face of difficulty, patience, endurance, fortitude, steadfastness, perseverance."[12]

- **"Patience"** (NIV, NRSV), "longsuffering" (KJV) is *makrothymia*, the "state of remaining tranquil while awaiting an outcome, patience, steadfastness, endurance."[13]

The words are similar. According to Trench, "*Hupomonē* is remaining under difficulties without succumbing, while *makrothumia* is the long endurance that does not retaliate."[14]

Two other qualities are joyfulness and giving thanks. All these qualities are marks of a disciple. All these qualities are the subject of Paul's prayer for the Colossian church. How do you measure up? Are you growing in these qualities?

---

[12] *Hypomonē*, BDAG 1039, 1.
[13] *Makrothymia*, BDAG 612, 1.
[14] Richard Chenevix Trench, *Synonyms of the New Testament* (1880), cited by Robertson, *Word Pictures*, in loc.

Q2. (Colossians 1:9-12a) What are the elements of Paul's prayer for the Colossian believers? What are the seven or eight specific results that he prays will be produced in their lives? Which of these are most important in a Christian disciple? Which, you think, are least important? What happens when some are missing?
http://www.joyfulheart.com/forums/index.php?showtopic=957

Dominion of Darkness, Kingdom of Light (1:12-13)

Now Paul moves from prayer to praise. He has recounted how he has prayed for the Colossian believers. Now he praises God for the dramatic nature of their salvation.

> "12 ... Joyfully giving thanks to the Father who has qualified you to share in the inheritance of the saints in [the kingdom of[15]] light. 13 For he has rescued us from the **dominion** of darkness and brought us into the **kingdom** of the Son he loves." (1:12-13)

Paul describes their salvation in almost cosmic terms – dominion and kingdom. Let's define the words and then look at the implications of this characterization.

"Dominion" (NIV), **"power"** (NRSV, KJV) is *exousia*. The word originally referred to "freedom of choice," that is, "the 'right' to act, decide, or dispose of one's property as one wishes," then "potential or resource to command, control, or govern." Here it refers to "the sphere in which power is exercised, domain."[16] The word is sometimes used in lists of spiritual powers in both Colossians (1:16; 2:10; 2:15) and Ephesians (1:21; 3:10), usually used alongside "principalities" (KJV) or "rulers" and translated "power" or "authority." It's most famous occurrence is in Paul's classic passage on spiritual warfare and putting on the full armor of God:

---

[15] The words "the kingdom of" in verse 13 are not in the Greek text, but added by the NIV to fill out the idea. I don't think these words "the kingdom of light" are called for – though they provide an antithesis to "dominion of darkness." But the meaning of the passage isn't distorted by the NIV's addition.

[16] *Exousia*, BDAG 353, 6. There are a couple of similar usages in Luke 22:53 ("the power of darkness"), Luke 23:7 ("Herod's jurisdiction"), and Ephesians 2:2 ("the power of the air").

"For our struggle is not against flesh and blood, but against the rulers, against the **authorities**, against the powers of this dark world and against the spiritual forces of evil in the heavenly realms." (Ephesians 6:12)

We'll consider these evil spiritual forces further as we study Colossians.

"Kingdom" is the contrasting authority structure, the word always used to refer to the "kingdom of God" or "kingdom of heaven" in the New Testament. The word is *basileia*, which can refer to "the act of ruling" – "kingship, royal power, royal rule," usually "the kingdom of God" or "royal reign of God," or, sometimes, "territory ruled by a king, kingdom."[17]

Look at the contrasts between these two domains:

Satan's realm	God's realm
Darkness (1:13)	Light (1:12)
	Love (1:13)
	Redemption, forgiveness (1:14)

We tend to take these concepts figuratively rather than acknowledging the existence of these contrasting spiritual realms, but they are real. One is dark, malignant, and controlling. The other is filled with light, hope, love, redemption, and forgiveness. Dear friends, this is the spiritual issue of our world. In Christ, we offer light, life, and hope to people who are in spiritual bondage. Will we love them enough to care and lead them to the light?

[17] *Basileia*, BDAG 168, 1bδ.

Q3. (Colossians 1:12-13) Why does Paul use the terms darkness and light to portray his readers past and future? Why does he remind them where they came from? What is "the inheritance of the saints in light" that he mentions? In verse 13 we find two terms used of governing bodies? How are they contrasted in verse 13? In what sense are subjects "governed" in each?

http://www.joyfulheart.com/forums/index.php?showtopic=958

The Father's Salvation (1:12-14)

We've looked at the two spiritual realms. Now read the passage again, with an eye to the action verbs and ideas that characterize God's salvation in Christ:

"12 ... The Father who has qualified you to share in the inheritance of the saints in the kingdom of light. 13 For he has rescued us from the dominion of darkness and brought us into the kingdom of the Son he loves, 14 in whom we have redemption, the forgiveness of sins." (1:12-14)

1. Qualified

2. Rescued

3. Brought us into the Kingdom

4. Redeemed

5. Forgiven

Let's take time to examine these concepts one at a time – even if you already think you know what they mean.

1. **"Qualified"** (NIV), "enabled" (NRSV), "made meet" (KJV) is *hikanoō*, "to cause to be adequate, make sufficient, qualify," perhaps shading into the sense "empower, authorize."[18] The word is used only here and in 2 Corinthians 3:6 ("made us competent as ministers"). We don't "accept Christ" of our own volition. We aren't masters of our fate. We can only come to God because of his own favor

---

[18] *Hikanoō*, BDAG 473. Liddell-Scott sees a passive use in classical Greek, "be empowered" (*PTeb.* 20.8).

and mercy – God's grace. He – and he alone – has allowed us to approach him. We have no standing on our own to appear before God. Our qualification is our union with Christ, God's beloved Son.

2. **"Rescued"** (NIV, NRSV), "delivered" (KJV) is *rhyomai*, "to rescue from danger, save, rescue, deliver, preserve someone."[19] Rescue involves giving aid to someone who is so endangered that they are unable to save themselves from death. A hand reaches out and grasps the drowning woman and pulls her to safety. A shepherd's crook helps extract a panicked sheep from a thicket in which it has become entangled – and is helpless prey to predators. Salvation is not a "helping hand" to assist a person over the bumps of life. It is a "saving hand" to pull a helpless person to safety.

3. **"Brought"** (NIV), **"transferred"** (NRSV), "translated" (KJV) is *methistēmi*, "transfer from one place to another, remove."[20] This talks about a transfer of citizenship from the dominion of darkness to the kingdom of God's dear son. This is not a gradual evolution, but an abrupt event, using the Aorist tense. Jesus taught a similar concept:

> "I tell you the truth, whoever hears my word and believes him who sent me has eternal life and will not be condemned; he has crossed over[21] from death to life." (John 5:24)

> "We know that we have passed from death to life, because we love our brothers." (1 John 3:14a)

4. **"Redemption"** is *apolytrōsis*. Originally the word meant, "buying back" a slave or captive, that is, "making free" by payment of a ransom. Here is means, "release from a captive condition, release, redemption, deliverance."[22] The implication is that we were in slavery, in bondage, unable to help ourselves. But Jesus' death on the cross paid the price for our manumission, our purchase.[23] Paul says, "Do

---

[19] *Rhyomai*, BDAG 902.

[20] *Methistēmi*, BDAG 625, 1a. This is a compound verb, from *meta*, "exchange, transfer, transmutation" + *histēmi*, "set, stand, place."

[21] *Metabainō*, "to change from one state or condition to another state, pass, pass on" (BDAG 638, 2a).

[22] *Apolytrōsis*, BDAG 117, 2a.

[23] Note that the phrase "through his blood" (KJV) is omitted by modern translations, since it appears in only a few late manuscripts.

you not know that your body is a temple of the Holy Spirit.... You are not your own; you were bought at a price." (1 Corinthians 6:19-20)

5. **"Forgiveness"** is *áphesis*. Originally the word meant, "the act of freeing and liberating from something that confines, release" from captivity. By extension it means here, "the act of freeing from an obligation, guilt, or punishment, pardon, cancellation."[24] Think about it for a moment: You have been forgiven of all your sins! It is a free and complete pardon! Praise God!

Q4. (Colossians 1:12-13) What are the three or four action verbs in verses 12 and 13 that paint a picture of salvation? Who performs the action? Who is it performed on? In what way were we "qualified/enabled/made meet"? In what way were we "rescued" or "delivered"?

http://www.joyfulheart.com/forums/index.php?showtopic=959

Q5. (Colossians 1:13-14) What are the two qualities mentioned in verse 14 that characterize the "kingdom of his beloved Son"? What did the idea of redemption mean in the Greek? In what way did Christ "redeem" us? What is the significance of the fact that our sins are forgiven in this kingdom?

http://www.joyfulheart.com/forums/index.php?showtopic=960

This has been a wonderful start to a power-packed epistle:

- A thumbnail of Epaphras, an ideal Christian worker

---

[24] *Aphesis*, BDAG 155, 2.

- An apostle's prayer for spiritual growth
- The profile of Christian character that is forming in us
- A 5-fold description of the amazing salvation we have been given.

In it all we have cause for rejoicing and hope for the future.

Prayer

Father, thank you for your rich love for us. Thank you for your hope that can see beyond our faults to your plan for us and your character that is growing within us. Thank you for not giving up on us. Thank you for Jesus' mighty act of salvation on the cross. In his name, we pray. Amen.

Key Verses

"All over the world this gospel is bearing fruit and growing, just as it has been doing among you since the day you heard it and understood God's grace in all its truth." (Colossians 1:6, NIV)

"For he has rescued us from the dominion of darkness and brought us into the kingdom of the Son he loves, in whom we have redemption, the forgiveness of sins." (Colossians 1:13-14, NIV)

2. The Supremacy of Christ (Colossians 1:15-19)

How is Jesus seen in the culture around us?

- As a great teacher.

- As the founder of a major world religion.

- As a healer and miracle worker.

- As a great man.

Each of these describes Jesus accurately. But each falls short – very far short – of who he really is.

In this lesson, Paul explodes a merely human understanding of Jesus. He speaks of Jesus Christ in cosmic terms. If what he says is true, then Christ is worthy of our awe and worship and service. If it is not true,

Christ Pantokrator, 12th century Byzantine mosaic, dome of La Martorana, Palermo (Santa Maria dell'Ammiraglio, *Saint Mary of the Admiral*).

Jesus remains just a man. Let's examine these audacious claims for who Jesus is.

But first we need to set this letter in its proper context. As we discussed in the introduction, Colossians seems to have been written with two purposes in mind:

1. To encourage and ground this relatively new Christian community, and

2. To keep them from the seduction of false teachers, probably from a variety of mystical Judaism that tended to denigrate these Gentile Christians' faith in Christ in favor of the claims of Judaism.

Paul's answer to both needs is to help open their vision of who Christ is: his greatness and preeminence. If the Christians understand better who they have in Christ, any other religion loses its luster. In Christ alone they are fulfilled. They are complete in him.

Hymn to Christ (1:15-20)

The passage we'll be looking at next is *the* classic passage in the New Testament that can help us understand more clearly who Christ is. It is at the apex of Christology, the knowledge of Christ. I encourage you to pause and to read aloud these verses so your ears can hear the power of these words. Let them sink into your soul.

> "15 He is the image of the invisible God, the firstborn over all creation. 16 For by him all things were created: things in heaven and on earth, visible and invisible, whether thrones or powers or rulers or authorities; all things were created by him and for him. 17 He is before all things, and in him all things hold together. 18 And he is the head of the body, the church; he is the beginning and the firstborn from among the dead, so that in everything he might have the supremacy.
>
> 19 For God was pleased to have all his fullness dwell in him, 20 and through him to reconcile to himself all things, whether things on earth or things in heaven, by making peace through his blood, shed on the cross. (1:15-20)

We'll cover verses 15 to 19 of the hymn in this lesson, and consider Christ's reconciliation in the next lesson.

Christian Hymns in New Testament Letters

This passage seems to be a hymn or poem inserted into Paul's letter to the Colossians. Whether it is of his own composition or a hymn of anonymous authorship circulating among the churches of the first century we don't know – nor does it matter. The passage is "skillfully worded and rhythmically balanced, deserving to be called a poem."[1]

Throughout the New Testament epistles we occasionally see evidence of poems that can be recognized by several earmarks:

1. The flow of the letter seems to be interrupted at these points.

2. The style is elevated and differs from the normal prose of the letter.

3. They are set off by introductory phrases that indicate a change (here, the relative pronoun "who"),

4. They tend to set up a contrast, and

---

[1] Wright, *Colossians*, p. 68.

5.   The vocabulary tends to be rare and highly stylized.[2]

In addition to our passage, we see examples of early hymns and poems in Ephesians 5:14; Philippians 2:6-11; 1 Timothy 3:16; and 2 Timothy 2:11-13. Our passage is not only profound in what it reveals about Christ, it is a beautiful literary gem in its own right.

Our passage contains two parts. First, seven different cameos that highlight various aspects of Christ's supremacy (verses 15-18) and second, an explanation of how God fulfills his purpose through Christ (verses 19-20).

1. Image of the Invisible God (1:15a)

Let's begin our mediation on this passage with the first cameo:

"He is the image of the invisible God...." (1:15a)

This phrase introduces two contrasting concepts: image and invisibility. An image is something you can see. Invisibility, by definition, you can't see.[3] The great glory of Judaism was its belief in one God who could not be seen. In fact, the Ten Command-ments prohibit any kind of carved image of God, such as the idols that were so common in the ancient world. The people of Israel were to know God as a spiritual being, not as a physical being. Indeed, Jesus declared, "God is spirit" (John 4:24). This understanding of God's invisibility is part of the Christian understanding of God, as well.

"God's **invisible** qualities – his eternal power and divine nature...." (Romans 1:20)

"Now to the King eternal, immortal, **invisible**, the only God...." (1 Timothy 1:17)

"[Moses] persevered because he saw him who is **invisible**." (Hebrews 11:27)

The amazing truth of Christianity is that the invisible God has allowed himself to be seen in Jesus of Nazareth. The word "image" is *eikōn*, "an object shaped to resemble the form or appearance of something, 'likeness, portrait,' then figuratively, by extension, "that which has the same form as something else (not a crafted object), 'living image.'"[4] John's Gospel especially ponders this paradox:

"The Word became flesh and made his dwelling among us. We have seen his glory, the glory of the One and Only, who came from the Father, full of grace and truth....

---

[2] Ralph P. Martin, "Hymns, Hymn Fragments, Songs, Spiritual Songs," DPL 419-423, citing E. Stauffer, *New Testament Theology* (Macmillan, 1956).

[3] "Invisible" is *aoratos*, " pertaining to not being subject to being seen, unseen, invisible," from *a-*, "not" + *oraō*, "to see" (BDAG 94).

[4] *Eikōn*, BDAG 283, 2.

No one has ever seen God, but God the One and Only, who is at the Father's side, has made him known." (John 1:14, 18)

"Philip said, 'Lord, show us the Father and that will be enough for us.' Jesus answered: 'Don't you know me, Philip, even after I have been among you such a long time? Anyone who has seen me has seen the Father.'" (John 14:8-9)

John's Gospel is clear that the Father and Son are different Persons, but that in the Son, God can be seen in all his glory. Amazing!

Q1. (Colossians 1:15a, 19) The great understanding of Judaism was that God is spirit, not physical. That he is invisible. Any idol that tries to depict him is blasphemous. So what is the significance of the statement that Jesus is "the image of the invisible God"? According to verse 19, to what degree does this image accurately represent God? Is Jesus actually God in the flesh, or only a manifestation of God, a kind of holograph?*
http://www.joyfulheart.com/forums/index.php?showtopic=961

*A holograph might be like Princess Leia in Star Wars sending a message through R2-D2: "Help me Obi-Wan Kenobi, you're my only hope...."

---

2. Firstborn Over All Creation (1:15b-16)

The second cameo of Christ in this hymn is as Creator.

"15 He is ... the firstborn over all creation. 16 For by him all things were created: things in heaven and on earth, visible and invisible, whether thrones or powers or rulers or authorities; all things were created by him and for him." (1:15b-16)

This verse uses the Near Eastern concept of "firstborn" (*prōtotokos*). "Firstborn" can suggest both birth order (as in 1:18b) and the special status accorded the firstborn son, as in our verse.[5] "Firstborn over all creation" doesn't mean that Jesus is the first created being, but that he is preeminent over all created beings. A couple of Old Testament references show this use of the concept of "firstborn" as preeminent:

"Then say to Pharaoh, 'This is what the LORD says: Israel is my firstborn son.'" (Exodus 4:22)

---

[5] *Prōtotokos*, BDAG 894, 2a.

"I will also appoint him my firstborn,
the most exalted of the kings of the earth." (Psalms 89:27)

So Jesus is "the firstborn over all creation," the sum total of everything created. Verse 16 uses the verb "create," *ktizō*, "to bring something into existence, create."[6] But the author isn't talking about the fauna and flora of the earth so much as sentient beings, both human beings and spiritual beings (see verse 23), for he continues:

"For by him all things were created:
things in heaven and on earth,
visible and invisible,
whether thrones or powers
or rulers or authorities;
all things were created by him and for him. (1:16)

The Jewish opponents of the church in Colossae apparently practiced angel worship (2:18), as did the Jews opposed in the Letter to the Hebrews (Hebrews 1:4-14). They saw Jesus as human, not divine. But this Christian hymn states that Jesus is the Creator of all these lesser spiritual beings. He is above them all. In fact, they were created to serve him ("for him").

Later Gnosticism saw God as separated from human beings by a series of emanations of God, spiritual beings that were in between. The Bible is clear. Jesus, whom we serve, is their Master and Creator and is over them all.

In Lesson 1 we compared the "dominion of darkness" to the "kingdom of God's dear Son." Paul mentioned in Ephesians:

"For our struggle is not against flesh and blood, but against the rulers (*archē*), against the authorities (*exousia*), against the powers (*kosmokratōr*) of this dark world and against the spiritual forces of evil in the heavenly realms." (Ephesians 6:12)

In our passage he refers to a few of these levels of spiritual authority, probably referring to fallen angels, now in the demonic sphere:

"... Whether thrones or powers or rulers (*archē*) or authorities (*exousia*)." (1:16)

There's been a lot of speculation, especially in medieval times, about the exact nature of these ruling powers. But we don't know more than the Scripture tells us:

---

[6] *Ktizō*, BDAG 572.

- **"Thrones"** refers to the seat of authority, and the power who sits on such a throne.[7]

- **"Powers"** (NIV), "dominions" (NRSV, KJV) is the plural of *kyriotēs*, the majestic power which is wielded by the *kyrios*, the lord and master.[8]

- **"Rulers"** (NIV, NRSV), "principalities" (KJV) is *archē*, "an authority figure who initiates activity or process, ruler, authority."[9] The word also occurs in Ephesians 6:12 quoted above, and at 2:10, 15, which describe Christ's power and victory over them.

- **"Authorities"** (NIV), "powers" (NRSV, KJV) is *exousia*, "bearer of ruling authority."[10]

This passage ends with the words, "All things were created **by him** and **for him**" (1:16e). Jesus is not just one among various spiritual authorities. He is the Creator of them all and they exist to serve him.

---

[7] *Thronos* (from which we get our word "throne") is "chair, seat," a chair set aside for one of high status, "throne," then, by extension, the power or person of the one who sits on the throne, "supreme power over a political entity, dominion, sovereignty" or "the enthroned" (BDAG 460, 2 and 3).

[8] *Kyriotēs* is "the essential nature of the *kyrios*, especially, the majestic power that the *kyrios* wields, "ruling power, lordship, dominion" (BDAG 579, 3). The primary meaning of the adjective *kyrios* relates to possession of power or authority, in various senses: "strong, authoritative, valid, ruling"; then to that which is preeminently important principal, essential. As a noun it refers to "one who is in a position of authority, lord, master" (BDAG 577).

[9] *Archē*, BDAG 137, 6.

[10] The basic idea of *exousia* is a state of control over something, "freedom of choice, right." The word is widely used of governmental offices and individuals. Here, "bearer of ruling authority" (BDAG 353, 5b).

Q2. (Colossians 1:15b-17) What does "firstborn of all creation/every creature" mean? Is Jesus a created being? If not, what does "firstborn" mean here? What do verses 16-17 teach about Jesus' pre-existence? What does verse 16b teach about the purpose of creation? According to verse 17, what is Jesus' past role in creation? What is his present role in creation?

http://www.joyfulheart.com/forums/index.php?showtopic=962

Q3. (Colossians 1:16) "Thrones," "powers," "rulers," "principalities," "authorities," etc. probably refer to both earthly as well as angelic and demonic dominions. What does this passage teach about the relation of these powers to Jesus? How should this affect our fear of them? How should it affect our prayers?

http://www.joyfulheart.com/forums/index.php?showtopic=963

---

3. Before All Things (1:17a)

The third cameo of Christ in this passage is found in verse 17a:

"He is before all things...." (1:17)

The Greek word "before" is *pro*, a "marker of a point of time prior to another point of time, earlier than, before."[11] This passage teaches the pre-existence of Christ. He is not just a human, nor a created being himself. He predates everything. We see this taught throughout the New Testament:

---

[11] *Pro*, BDAG 864, 2.

> "**In the beginning** was the Word, and the Word was with God, and the Word was God. He was with God **in the beginning**. Through him all things were made; without him nothing was made that has been made." (John 1:1-3)

> "'I tell you the truth,' Jesus answered, '**before Abraham was born, I am!**'" (John 8:58)

> "And now, Father, glorify me in your presence with the glory I had with you **before the world began**." (John 17:5)

Jesus is the "I AM," the eternally existent God, "who was, and is, and is to come" (Revelation 4:8). We see a similar idea in verse 18b, where Christ is spoken of as "the beginning."

4. In Him All Things Hold Together (1:17b)

There is a fourth cameo in verse 17b:

> "... In him all things hold together." (1:17)

"Hold together" (NIV, NRSV), "consist" (KJV) is *synistēmi*, originally, "to bring together by gathering, unite, collect." As an intransitive verb it is sometimes used as "to be composed or compounded of various parts, consist" (as in the KJV), but also, "to come to be in a condition of coherence, continue, endure, exist, hold together."[12] This word also occurs in 2 Peter:

> "... Long ago by God's word the heavens existed and the earth was formed (*synistēmi*) out of water and by water." (2 Peter 3:5)

See also:

> "When the earth and all its people quake,
> it is I who hold its pillars firm." (Psalms 75:3)

> "The Son is the radiance of God's glory and the exact representation of his being, **sustaining**[13] **all things** by his powerful word." (Hebrews 1:3a)

The implications of this are that Jesus is not just the clockmaker who creates the timepiece and sets it in motion and then leaves it. He is one who continually sustains it and holds it together, despite all the forces – both subatomic and large-scale – that might blow it apart.

---

[12] *Synistēmi*, BDAG 973, B3.

[13] "Sustaining" (NIV, NRSV), "upholding" (KJV) is *pherō*, "bear, carry," here with the specific meaning, "to cause to continue in a state or condition, sustain" (BDAG 1051, 5).

5. Head of the Body, the Church (1:18a)

"And he is the head of the body, the church...." (1:18a)

Paul refers to the head-body analogy, which he develops more thoroughly in the next chapter, where he refers to an opponent of the Colossian church:

"He has lost connection with the Head, from whom the whole body, supported and held together by its ligaments and sinews, grows as God causes it to grow." (Colossians 2:19)

We'll consider the analogy more thoroughly later.

"Head" is *kephalē*. It means first, the physical head, particularly in the head-body analogy. But then extends to a figurative use as "being of high status, head." With living beings, *kephalē* refers to superior rank.[14] We see this use later in the letter without the head-body analogy:

"... Christ, who is the head over every power and authority." (2:10)

But in our passage in 1:18a, the emphasis is on Christ's vital connection to and authority over the church. We are Christ's body here on earth and serve under his direction. The point is that Christ not only has priority over the principalities and powers, he is the supreme Head of the church itself.

Q4. (Colossians 1:18) How should the assertion that Jesus is the "head of the body, the church" affect the way we conceive of the church? Is he talking about the universal church or a local congregation, or both? If we believe that Jesus is the head of the church, how should that affect the way we conduct our life and ministry as the church? In what ways does the visible church represent the "head"? How well do we as the body follow his leadership?

http://www.joyfulheart.com/forums/index.php?showtopic=964

---

[14] *Kephalē*, BDAG 541-542.

6. The Beginning (1:18b)

In addition to the concept of Christ's preexistence ("he is before all things"), Paul emphasis Christ as "the beginning":

> "He is the beginning and the firstborn from among the dead, so that in everything he might have the supremacy." (1:18)

"Beginning" is *archē*. The basic idea of the word, however, is not "ruler" (as in verse 16), but "the commencement of something as an action, process, or state of being, beginning, that is, a point of time at the beginning of a duration." Here, in context with "firstborn," Paul is speaking figuratively of a person, "one with whom a process begins, beginning."[15] At the close of Revelation, Jesus says:

> "I am the Alpha and the Omega, the **First** and the Last, the **Beginning** and the End." (Revelation 22:13)

Christ shares this title with God the Father (Revelation 21:6).

7. Firstborn from Among the Dead (1:18c)

Next, this hymn of Christ speaks of his resurrection:

> "He is ... the firstborn from among the dead." (1:18c)

In verse 15b, "firstborn" was used in the sense of primacy due to birth order. Here, the idea of birth order itself is in view. Jesus is "firstborn from among the dead" here and in Revelation 1:5 in the sense that he is the first to be resurrected from the dead. His resurrection from the dead encourages us that we, too, will be raised at his coming. He is our hope.

> "**I am the resurrection** and the life. He who believes in me will live, even though he dies; and whoever lives and believes in me will never die." (John 11:25-26)

> "The prophets and Moses said ... that the Christ would suffer and, as the **first to rise from the dead**, would proclaim light to his own people and to the Gentiles." (Acts 26:22-23)

> "But Christ has indeed been raised from the dead, the **firstfruits** of those who have fallen asleep...." (1 Corinthians 15:20)

---

[15] *Archē*, BDAG 137, 2. The idea of ruler or authority, which we saw in 1:16b above as "rulers" (NIV) or "principalities" (KJV), derives from the concept of one who begins or initiates.

Preeminence (1:18d)

Christ's 7-fold distinctives outlined in this hymn culminate with a purpose clause (Greek *hina*):

"... So that in everything he might have the supremacy." (1:18d)

"Supremacy" (NIV), "supreme" (NJB), "first place" (NRSV, NASB), "preeminence" (KJV) is *prōteuō*, "to hold the highest rank in a group, be first, have first place."[16] Jesus wasn't given these distinctives to *make* him preeminent. Rather, these distinctives *demonstrate* his preeminence. He *is* in first place – above any person or any spiritual power, in all creation.

Fullness of God Dwells in Him (1:19)

The hymn has reached its high point in the supremacy of Christ over creation. Now it considers his relationship to God:

"For God was pleased to have all his **fullness** dwell[17] in him." (1:19)

"Fullness" is *plērōma*, "that which is brought to fullness or completion," here, "sum total, fullness," even "(super)abundance."[18] The word is used in second century Gnostic writings as a religious technical term, but here in Colossians it affirms that in Jesus, God is fully present and that Jesus is fully divine. This is used in a similar way in the next chapter (where we'll consider it in greater detail), as well as in Ephesians:

"[9] For in Christ all the **fullness** (*plērōma*) of the Deity lives in bodily form, [10] and you have been given **fullness** (*plēroō*) in Christ, who is the head over every power and authority." (Colossians 2:9-10)

"[I pray that you may] know this love that surpasses knowledge – that you may be filled to the measure of all the **fullness** of God." (Ephesians 3:19)

"... Until we all reach unity in the faith and in the knowledge of the Son of God and become mature, attaining to the whole measure of the **fullness** of Christ. " (Ephesians 4:13)

So who is Jesus? Is he a good teacher? A prophet? An example? Yes, all these things. But he is more. He is supreme and he is God in the flesh!

---

[16] *Prōteuō*, BDAG 892.

[17] "Dwell" is *katoikeō*," to live in a locality for any length of time, live, dwell, reside, settle (down)" (BDAG 534, 1b).

[18] *Plērōma*, BDAG 828, 3b.

Prayer

Father, thank you for sending your best to us. I'm ashamed when I realize afresh who Christ actually is compared to how we welcomed him, treated him shamefully, and then put him on display on the cross as an example of how we treat God in our midst. Forgive us. Let Christ be supreme in us and all God's children. In Jesus' name, I pray. Amen.

Key Verse

"For by him all things were created: things in heaven and on earth, visible and invisible, whether thrones or powers or rulers or authorities; all things were created by him and for him. He is before all things, and in him all things hold together." (Colossians 1:16-17, NIV)

3. Christ the Reconciler (Colossians 1:20-23)

We've looked at Christ in all his glory. Now we turn to his mission: reconciliation. The Christian hymn in verses 15-20 has two parts: (1) who Jesus is (verses 15-19) and (2) what Jesus has done (verses 19-20). Verse 19 begins that second part by explaining that God dwells fully within Jesus. Through Jesus then, God reconciles the world to himself by making peace with mankind on the cross. Let's focus in on this way of looking at salvation.

Reconcile All Things to God (1:20a)

"For God was pleased[1] ... through him to reconcile to himself all things, whether things on earth or things in heaven" (1:20b)

"Reconcile" is *apokatallassō*. This compound Greek word in verses 20 and 21 is found only in

Carl Heinrich Bloch (Danish painter, 1834-1890), "Consolator" altarpiece, oil on canvas.

Christian writings. It is formed from *apo-*, "finishing and completion" + *katallassō*, "the exchange of hostility for a friendly relationship, reconcile" – "to reconcile completely."[2]

Whom does God reconcile? "All things, whether things on earth or things in heaven," Paul tells us. It means estranged human beings, certainly. But does it refer also to evil spiritual forces – the principalities and powers, for example? Perhaps some of them, though Revelation tells us that the ultimate destiny of Satan, the Antichrist, and the false prophet are the lake of fire (Revelation 20:10). In Ephesians, Paul states God's purpose as:

"... To bring all things in heaven and on earth together under one head, even Christ." (Ephesians 1:10)

In Philippians we see Christ's final exaltation over all:

[1] "Pleased" is *eudokeō*, "to consider something as good and therefore worthy of choice, consent, determine, resolve" (BDAG 404, 1).
[2] *Apokatallassō*, Thayer.

" Therefore God exalted him to the highest place
and gave him the name that is above every name,
that at the name of Jesus every knee should bow,
in heaven and on earth and under the earth,
and every tongue confess that Jesus Christ is Lord,
to the glory of God the Father." (Philippians 2:9-11)

Making Peace through His Blood (1:20b)

"Reconcile ... by making peace through his blood, shed on the cross." (1:20b)

The Greek text lacks the word "shed" added by the NIV to clarify the idea, though I don't think the NIV distorts the meaning. The text reads, "by making peace through the blood of his cross" (Colossians 1:20, NRSV).

How does shed blood bring peace? Paul states it as a fact, as a kind of shorthand for the gospel, but doesn't spell out the rationale for his statement here. However, in a nutshell, here it is:

1. **Enemies.** Because of our sins and self-centeredness we have made ourselves enemies of God (Romans 5:10). We both resist God's will in our hearts (Romans 8:7) and our sins and unholiness separate us from the Holy God (Isaiah 59:2).

2. **Sacrifice.** When Jesus died on the cross and shed his blood, he did so as a sacrifice for our sins (Romans 3:25; 1 Corinthians 5:7).

3. **Love.** This unilateral act of love astounds us and draws us to Jesus (Romans 5:8; 1 John 4:19).

4. **Faith.** When we put our trust in Jesus, repent, and ask forgiveness, we are reconciled to God (Ephesians 2:8-9).

Now we are at a state of peace with God. We are no longer enemy combatants who resist him, but enemies whom he has won over and transformed into his friends by his own mercy and grace.

Alienation Contrasted with Reconciliation (1:21-22)

Now Paul spells out the contrast:

"21 Once you were alienated from God and were enemies in your minds because of your evil behavior. 22 But now he has reconciled you by Christ's physical body through death to present you holy in his sight, without blemish and free from accusation." (1:21-22)

Look at the descriptive words which describe our previous condition:

- **"Alienated"** (NIV, KJV), **"estranged"** (NRSV) is *apallotrioō*, "estrange, alienate", from *apo-*, "from" (as in "separation, liberation, cessation, departure") + *allotrios*, "belonging to another, foreign, strange."[3]

- **"Enemies"** (NIV, KJV), **"hostile"** (NRSV) is the adjective *echthros*, "pertaining to being hostile, hating," or as a substantive, "enemy."[4]

Then contrast these with the amazing words that describe our new condition granted through God's grace alone:

- **"Reconciled"** which we examined above in verse 20.

- **"Holy"** is *hagios*. Here it means, "consecrated to God, holy, pure, reverent."[5]

- **"Without blemish"** (NIV), "blameless" (NRSV), "unblameable" (KJV) is *amōmos*, initially, "pertaining to being without defect or blemish, unblemished," from *a-*, "not" + *mōmos*, "blemish, blot, disgrace." It is used in the Old and New Testaments of the absence of defects in sacrificial animals. Then, by extension, "pertaining to being without fault and therefore morally blameless."[6] It is difficult to think of ourselves in this way, but this is how God has made us to be in Christ.

- **"Free from accusation"** (NIV), "irreproachable" (NRSV), "unreproveable" (KJV) is *anenklētos*, "blameless, irreproachable,"[7] from *a-*, "not" + *enkaleō*, "to call in, to call to account, bring a charge against, accuse." The word is also used in 1 Corinthians 1:8 and as qualifications for elders (1 Timothy 3:10) and overseers (Titus 1:6-7).

---

[3] *Apallotrioō*, BDAG 96.
[4] *Echthros*, BDAG 419, 2a or b.
[5] *Hagios*, BDAG 10, 1aβ Aleph.
[6] *Amōmos*, BDAG 56, 2a. See similar statements in Ephesians 1:4; 5:27; 2 Peter 3:14; Philippians 2:15; Jude 24.
[7] *Anenklētos*, BDAG 76.

The key phrase here is "... in his sight." (1:22). In our own sight we are sinners, seemingly unable to live consistently free of sin. But God sees us as united with Christ. Thus we are seen "in him," not on our own.

Q1. (Colossians 1:20-22). What does "reconcile" mean? What was our state before reconciliation? (verse 21)
 http://www.joyfulheart.com/forums/index.php?showtopic=965

Q2. (Colossians 1:20-22) By what means did Jesus accomplish this reconciliation? What does "the blood of his cross" have to do with it? What is the purpose of this reconciliation? (verse 22) To whom are we "presented?" (verse 22)
http://www.joyfulheart.com/forums/index.php?showtopic=966

Q3. (Colossians 1:22) How can we be presented "holy," "without blemish," and "free from accusation" since we are not perfect? How is this possible?
http://www.joyfulheart.com/forums/index.php?showtopic=967

If You Continue (1:23)

Our salvation is not independent of Christ, but is very much "in him." Thus Paul warns us of the necessary condition of our salvation:

> "... If you continue in your faith, established and firm, not moved from the hope held out in the gospel." (1:23a)

In the face of the way the doctrine of Eternal Security is sometimes taught, this verse is troubling. Let's examine the words, then look at the implications.

- **"Continue"** is *epimenō*, "to continue in an activity or state, continue, persist (in), persevere,"[8] from *epi-*, "continuance, rest, influence upon or over"[9] + *menō*, "remain, stay, persist."

- **"Established"** (NIV), "securely established" (NRSV), "grounded" (KJV) is *themelioō*, "to provide a base for some material object or structure, lay a foundation," here used figuratively, "to provide a secure basis for the inner life and its resources, establish, strengthen."[10]

- **"Firm"** (NIV), "steadfast" (NRSV), "settled" (KJV) is *hedraios*, "pertaining to being firmly or solidly in place, firm, steadfast,"[11] from *hedra*, "seat, chair."

- **"Not moved"** (NIV, KJV), "not shifting" (NRSV) is the negative particle and the word *metakineō*, "shift, remove,"[12] from *meta-*, "exchange, transfer, transmutation" + *kineō*, "to cause to go, set in motion" (from which we get our English word "kinetics").

I'm not trying to exalt Calvinism as the peak of all theological understanding, but to clarify an important point that is sometimes forgotten. John Calvin taught the Perseverance of the Saints, that is, that the true believers do indeed continue in Christ and do not ultimately fall away. In the face of the persecutions of the end time, Jesus himself said, "the one who endures to the end will be saved" (Mark 13:13).

Contrast authentic Calvinism with a modern-day, cheap imitation, crudely known as "once saved, always saved." Some teach that if you've once prayed the sinner's prayer and been baptized, then you're saved, even if you later fall away and don't show any

---

[8] *Epimenō*, BDAG 375, 2.
[9] *Epi* in composition, Thayer, E1.
[10] *Themelioō*, BDAG 449, 2a.
[11] *Hedraios*, BDAG 276.
[12] *Metakineō*, BDAG 639.

signs of your Christian faith. Dear friends, this isn't biblical teaching, but a distortion of the holy truth. The Apostle Paul teaches clearly in our passage, "But now he has reconciled you ... if you continue in your faith..." (1:22-23a).

The true Christian faith is lived in union with Jesus, by faith in him, walking with him, receiving his encouragement and forgiveness throughout our lives.

> "God has given us eternal life, and this life is in his Son. He who has the Son has life;
> he who does not have the Son of God does not have life." (1 John 5:11-12)

Yes, we sin sometimes, but our heart is set on serving Christ, and his grace and his promises are our security.

Let's put this in context. The "hope" (*elpis*) has been offered the Colossian believers in the gospel that they originally heard through Epaphras. But now they are being enticed with another hope offered by the false teachers. Paul's aim is to enhance their confidence in Christ so they are no longer tempted by the hope of mystical Judaism. The rather stern warnings against drifting away that we see in the book of Hebrews are in the same context – to warn Christians that turning back to Judaism was to turn away from Christ (Hebrews 3:12-14; 6:4-8; 10:26-31). Our only hope, dear friends, is found in union with Christ – and this is the great and firm hope held out to us in the gospel.

The Hope of the Gospel (1:23)

Now Paul segues from salvation through Christ to a word about the gospel:

> "... Not moved from the hope held out in the gospel. This is the gospel that you heard and that has been proclaimed to every creature under heaven, and of which I, Paul, have become a servant." (1:23)

"Gospel," of course, is *euangelion*, "good news." The Greeks used the word for bringing news, especially of a victory or some other joyous event, in person or by letter. A runner, who would bring back news of a remarkable defeat of the enemy, was a bringer of good news. The word is used this way in the Old Testament:

> "How beautiful on the mountains
> are **the feet of those who bring good news,**
> who proclaim peace,
> who bring good tidings,
> who proclaim salvation,
> who say to Zion, 'Your God reigns!'" (Isaiah 52:7)

Jesus' message was called, "the gospel of the kingdom" (Matthew 4:23), that is, the good news that the Kingdom of God was at hand, that the Messiah is present to bring salvation. This is indeed good news! God has sent his Son to help us and rescue us!

Now Paul specifies this gospel in three ways:

> "This is the gospel that you heard and that has been proclaimed to every creature under heaven, and of which I, Paul, have become a servant." (1:23)

1. **You heard**. You Colossians received this very message of good news when you first became believers. It hasn't changed.

2. **Proclaimed**. The word "proclaimed" (NIV, NRSV), "preached" (KJV) is *kēryssō*, "to make public declarations, proclaim aloud."[13] Paul and other apostles and preachers have been proclaiming this gospel. It has been preached "to every creature under heaven," Paul says. Does he really mean that every person has heard the gospel? Probably not. Rather that the gospel has been proclaimed widely and openly. As Luke described Paul's ministry in Ephesus: "This went on for two years, so that all the Jews and Greeks who lived in the province of Asia heard the word of the Lord" (Acts 19:10).

3. **Served**. Third, Paul calls himself a "servant" (NIV, NRSV) or "minister" (KJV) of the gospel. The word is *diakonos* (from which we get our word "deacon"), "one who serves as an intermediary in a transaction, agent, intermediary, courier."[14] We are not free to teach any message that seems popular in our day. We are servants of the gospel, that is, our assigned job is to proclaim the good news.

---

[13] *Kēryssō*, BDAG 543, 2bβ.
[14] *Diakonos* BDAG 230, 1.

Q4. (Colossians 1:23) If our salvation depends upon the grace of God, not us, why is it necessary for us to "continue in your faith, established and firm, not moved"? What happens if we don't? What is the nature of the security we have in Jesus according to this text (and this text only*)?

*Please don't use proof texts from other verses in the New Testament, but interpret Colossians 1:23 in its appropriate context.

http://www.joyfulheart.com/forums/index.php?showtopic=968

We have examined the wonder of Christ's reconciliation of us, his former enemies. And we have seen the importance of commitment to our union with Christ, who is our hope. We are saved by Christ, and Christ alone. And it is to him that we trust our lives and our futures.

Prayer

Father, thank you for such a wonderful salvation. Thank you for the power of the One who has taken hold of us and rescued us. We don't deserve this, but we glory in it and in our Savior. In Jesus' name, we pray. Amen.

Key Verse

"But now he has reconciled you by Christ's physical body through death to present you holy in his sight, without blemish and free from accusation." (Colossians 1:22, NIV)

4. Paul's Labors for the Church (Colossians 1:24-2:5)

Paul began his letter with a prayer for the Colossians and a hymn that exalts the preeminence of Christ. Now he turns for a moment to describe his own ministry. Why?

The members of the Colossian church don't know him – except by reputation from afar. He is about to exhort them concerning both doctrine and faith. It is important that he establish before them that he is called to minister -- not only to the church at large – but also to them.

As we study this lesson, we begin to understand better our own call to ministry. No, we're not apostles, but we are certainly called to God's own purpose. Paul laid it all on the line. What must *we* undergo to serve Christ faithfully in our situations?

Rembrandt, "St. Paul in Prison" (1627). Oil on wood panel. 72.8 x 60.2 cm Staatsgalerie, Stuttgart, Germany.

A Servant of the Gospel and the Church (1:23, 25)

Paul introduces his ministry in the previous paragraph as he has exalted the gospel:

"This is the gospel that you heard and that has been proclaimed to every creature under heaven, and of which I, Paul, have become a servant." (1:23b)

Instead of exalting himself, he exalts the gospel and then introduces himself as a "servant" or "minister" of the gospel. The word is *diakonos* (which we saw in 1:7), from which we get our word "deacon." It means generally, "one who is busy with something in a manner that is of assistance to someone." Here it denotes, "one who serves as an intermediary in a transaction, agent, intermediary, courier."[1] In verse 25 he uses the same word in relationship to the church. Thus, we should think of ourselves as:

1. Servants of Christ (1:7, 4:7)
2. Servants of the gospel (1:23)
3. Servants of the church (1:25)

That's what you and I are, if we're faithful – agents, intermediaries, carriers of the gospel of Jesus Christ, for the sake of his church, his body. The message is primary; carrying it and spreading it is our mission.

Let me comment a moment on the third concept introduced in verse 25: servants of the church.

> "24b ... For the sake of his body, which is the church. 25 I have become its servant by the commission God gave me...." (1:24-25)

Are we servants of the church in the sense that it is our master? No. We are servants of the church by God's calling. God is our master, and caring for the church is his assignment for us. Sometimes churches, especially churches with a congregational form of government, tend to see its pastors as its employees. Certainly human accountability can be helpful. But it is important to know that pastors, as well as volunteer workers, serve the church on behalf of Christ, not primarily as hirelings of the church organization. We submit to one another, yes, but "out of reverence for Christ" (Ephesians 5:21). We don't serve Christ's church as "menpleasers" (3:22, KJV), but "work at it with all [our] heart, as working for the Lord, not for men" (3:23, NIV).

Suffering for You (1:24)

Now Paul turns to suffering – something that we'd rather not experience, but which is part of the ministry.

> "Now I rejoice in what was suffered for you, and I **fill up** in my flesh what is still lacking in regard to Christ's afflictions, for the sake of his body, which is the church." (1:24)

"Suffered/sufferings" is *pathēma*, from which we get our English words "pathos" and "pathetic." Here it means, "that which is suffered or endured, suffering, misfortune."[2] Paul's statement is remarkable in two ways. He makes two amazing claims:

---

[1] *Diakonos*, BDAG 230, 1.

1. To **complete in his body** what is lacking in Christ's sufferings. How could that be possible? and

2. To **suffer for the sake of the church**. How do your sufferings help the church?

First, Paul talks about filling up or supplementing. The rare double compound word *antanaplēroō* means to "take one's turn in filling up something,"[3] with the preposition *anti-* suggesting the idea "in turn."[4]

Of course, Christ's redemptive suffering on the cross for our atonement was complete and finished, "once and for all" (Romans 6:10; Hebrews 9:26-28). But that doesn't mean that Jesus is the last to suffer for the gospel. It was Christ's time to suffer on the cross. Now it is Paul's, and perhaps soon it will be yours.

Paul sees something still lacking in Christ's afflictions,[5] a "need, want, deficiency."[6] It's as if there's something preordained about this suffering. Consider the vision in Revelation:

> "When he opened the fifth seal, I saw under the altar the souls of those who had been slain because of the word of God and the testimony they had maintained. They called out in a loud voice, "How long, Sovereign Lord, holy and true, until you judge the inhabitants of the earth and avenge our blood?" Then each of them was given a white robe, and they were told to wait a little longer, **until the number** of their fellow servants and brothers who were to be killed as they had been **was completed** (*plēroō*)." (Revelation 6:9-11)

There's also a sense in which we are united with Christ in our sufferings. We share in his sufferings; *our* sufferings are a part of his.

> "We are ... heirs of God and co-heirs with Christ, if indeed we **share in his sufferings** in order that we may also share in his glory." (Romans 8:17-18)

---

[2] *Pathēma*, BDAG 247, 1.

[3] "Fill up" (NIV, KJV), "completing" (NRSV) is *antanaplēroō*, "take one's turn in filling up something," then, "fill up on one's part, supplement" (BDAG 87). This is a double compound word from *anti-*, "in turn" + *ana-*, "to, up to (the brim)" + *plēroō*, "to fill."

[4] Moo points out that *anti-* could suggest other ideas as well. Moo prefers the simple sense, "to fill up in order to complete" (Moo, *Colossians*, pp. 150-151).

[5] "Afflictions" is *thlipsis*. Originally it referred to physical "pressing, pressure." Here it is used metaphorically, "trouble that inflicts distress, oppression, affliction, tribulation" (BDAG 457, 1).

[6] "Lacking" (NIV, NRSV), "behind" (KJV) is *hysterēma*, "the lack of what is needed or desirable," frequently in contrast to abundance, "need, want, deficiency" (BDAG 104, 1).

"I want to know Christ ... and the **fellowship of sharing in his sufferings.**" (Philippians 3:10)

But more, Paul's sufferings in some way benefited the Colossian church – even the whole church. Look at verse 24 again:

"Now I rejoice in what was suffered **for you**, and I fill up in my flesh what is still lacking in regard to Christ's afflictions, **for the sake of his body, which is the church.**" (1:24)

The preposition "for," is used twice in verse 24 indicating "that an activity or event is in some entity's interest, for, in behalf of, for the sake of someone/something."[7] This idea is common in Paul's writings. For example:

"For we who are alive are always being given over to death for Jesus' sake, so that his life may be revealed in our mortal body. So then, death is at work in us, but **life is at work in you.**" (2 Corinthians 4:11-12)

"Therefore I endure everything for **the sake of the elect**, that they too may obtain the salvation that is in Christ Jesus, with eternal glory." (2 Timothy 2:10)

In what way do Paul's sufferings benefit the Church at Colossae – and us today?

1. **Inspiration.** Paul's example in suffering inspires us to endure as well.

2. **Accomplishment.** Paul's willingness to endure whatever is necessary to get the job done enables him to touch more lives. He doesn't quit when the going gets tough.

3. **Corporate unity and completeness.** Since both Paul and we are part of Christ's body, then Christ's sufferings affect us and our sufferings affect Christ. There will come a day when the last martyr is killed, the last suffering is done, and the afflictions of the Messiah will be complete.[8] Then Christ will return in glory. This is a more mystical idea, harder to get our head around, but I believe Paul has this in mind in verse 24.

---

[7] *Hyper*, BDAG 103, 1aε.

[8] Jewish literature speaks of the "messianic woes," tribulations to be endured by God's people in the days just preceding Messiah's coming (Moo, *Colossians*, p. 151).

> Q1. (Colossians 1:24) How could Paul's sufferings in prison complete what is lacking in Christ's afflictions? Is Paul referring to Christ's sufferings on the cross? Or is he seeing suffering in some kind of cosmic sense? If so, in what sense are your sufferings for Christ of value to the church?
>
> http://www.joyfulheart.com/forums/index.php?showtopic=969

Paul's Commission (1:25)

Now let's consider Paul's orders:

"I have become its servant by the **commission** God gave me **to present to you the word** of God in its fullness." (1:25)

Paul's calling is referred to here as a "commission" (NIV, NRSV), "dispensation" (KJV). The word is *oikonomia*, "responsibility of management, management of a household, direction, office."[9] His purpose is to declare the gospel fully – the "full gospel." "Present ... in its fullness" (NIV), "make fully known" (NRSV), "fulfill" (KJV) is *plēroō*, "to fulfill," the root of the word we discussed in verse 24 above. Here it connotes to "bring (the preaching of) the gospel to completion."[10]

The Mystery of Christ in You Gentiles (1:25-27)

Now Paul talks about the mystery contained in the gospel.

"[25] I have become its servant by the commission God gave me to present to you the word of God in its fullness – [26] the **mystery** that has been kept hidden for ages and generations, but is now disclosed to the saints. [27] To them God has chosen to make known among the Gentiles the glorious riches of this **mystery**, which is Christ in you, the hope of glory." (1:25-27)

"Mystery" in 1:26-27 and 2:2 is *mystērion*. Here Paul means by it, "the unmanifested or private counsel of God, (God's) secret."[11]

---

[9] *Oikonomia*, BDAG 697, 1b. Paul applies the idea of administration to the office of an apostle here and in 1 Corinthians 9:17 and Ephesians 3:2.

[10] *Plēroō*, BDAG 828, 3.

[11] *Mystērion*, BDB 662, 1b. This word refers to a "secret, secret rite, secret teaching, mystery," and was a religious technical term (used predominately in the plural, "mysteries"). In the Greco-Roman world it

What is the mystery? What about the gospel had been kept hidden,[12] only to be disclosed[13] in the time of the Messiah? The answer is clear: That Christ, the Messiah, would indwell not only the chosen Jewish people, but also the Gentiles who made up the bulk of the church at Colossae and elsewhere. It is a mystery overflowing with blessing to its recipients; Paul refers to its "glorious riches."[14] We Christians take God's blessing for granted. But for Gentile believers in the first century, who were being enticed to adopt Judaism, to realize that the Messiah came for them, too, was truly marvelous.

Christ in You, the Hope of Glory (1:27b)

I would like to explore and meditate further on verse 27:

> "To them God has chosen to make known among the Gentiles the glorious riches of this mystery, which is Christ in you, the hope of glory." (1:27)

In particular, I want to know, in what sense does Christ in us constitute our "hope of glory"? What does this mean?

"Glory" first appears in the Old Testament in the word *kābôd*, a word meaning "weightiness, honor," associated with the brilliant light and overwhelming splendor of God's presence "like a consuming fire" (Exodus 24:17). When Moses speaks to God, his face glows afterward in the afterglow of God's glory (Exodus 34:33-35). Angels of God wear brilliant white clothing with an appearance like lightning (Matthew 28:3). God is described as,

> "The blessed and only Ruler, the King of kings and Lord of lords, who alone is immortal and who **lives in unapproachable light**, whom no one has seen or can see." (1 Timothy 6:15-16)

The truly amazing mystery to me is that Christ in me is the hope of my own experience of and participation in God's glory, both now and in heaven. Consider these verses:

---

referred mostly to the mystery religions, with their secret teachings, religious and political in nature, concealed within many strange customs and ceremonies.

[12] "Kept hidden" (NIV), "hid" (KJV) is *apokryptō*, "to keep from being known, keep secret" (BDAG 114, 2).

[13] "Disclosed" (NIV), "revealed" (NRSV, KJV) is *phaneroō*, "to cause to become known, disclose, show, make known" (BDAG 104, 2aβ).

[14] "Riches" is *ploutos*, "riches, wealth," then more generally, "plentiful supply of something, a wealth, abundance" (BDAG 832, 2).

"And we, who with unveiled faces all reflect **the Lord's glory**, are being transformed into his likeness with **ever-increasing glory**, which comes from the Lord, who is the Spirit." (2 Corinthians 3:18)

"For our light and momentary troubles are achieving for us an **eternal glory** that far outweighs them all. So we fix our eyes not on what is seen, but on what is unseen. For what is seen is temporary, but what is unseen is eternal." (2 Corinthians 4:17-18)

"Now if we are children, then we are heirs – heirs of God and co-heirs with Christ, if indeed we share in his sufferings in order that we may also **share in his glory**." (Romans 8:17)

"When Christ, who is your life, appears, then you also will **appear with him in glory.**" (Colossians 3:4)

"These have come so that your faith – of greater worth than gold, which perishes even though refined by fire – may be proved genuine and may result in **praise, glory and honor** when Jesus Christ is revealed." (1 Peter 1:7)

"To the elders among you, I appeal as a fellow elder, a witness of Christ's sufferings and one who also will **share in the glory** to be revealed." (1 Peter 5:1)

"And the God of all grace, who called you to **his eternal glory** in Christ, after you have suffered a little while, will himself restore you and make you strong, firm and steadfast." (1 Peter 5:10)

I think of the African American spiritual, "This train is bound for glory, this train...." You and I have a hope ahead of being immersed in the presence and glory of God. And that hope springs from Christ dwelling in you now: "Christ in you, the hope of glory!"

Q2. (Colossians 1:26-27) What is the mystery that Paul talks about? In what sense was, "Christ in you, the hope of glory," hidden prior to this? In what sense is "glory" used here? What does "the hope of glory" mean in this context?
 http://www.joyfulheart.com/forums/index.php?showtopic=970

Present Everyone Perfect in Christ (1:28-29)

Paul has shared his vision – of the Gentiles experiencing the presence of Christ now and glory forever – he also shares in our passage (both here and in 2:2) the purposes that drive his ministry. Here's the first purpose statement:

> "28 We proclaim him, admonishing and teaching everyone with all wisdom, **so that** we may present everyone perfect in Christ. 29 To this end I labor, struggling with all his energy, which so powerfully works in me." (1:28-29)

Paul's purpose is to bring the Christians under his influence to maturity in Christ. The word translated "perfect" (NIV, KJV), "mature" (NRSV) is *teleios*. The word can mean, "perfect, pertaining to meeting the highest standard," or "pertaining to being mature, full-grown, mature, adult" or "pertaining to being fully developed in a moral sense."[15] We don't achieve complete perfection in this life. James reminds us:

> "We all stumble in many ways. If anyone is never at fault in what he says, he is a perfect man, able to keep his whole body in check." (James 3:2)

Nevertheless, we can come to a level of relative maturity in Christ. That is Paul's goal. When he presents[16] his converts and disciples to God as the fruit of his labor, he wants to be proud of them.

Verse 28 not only states Paul's final purpose. It also lays out his methods of achieving maturity:

---

[15] *Teleios*, BDAG 996, 1-4. The word was also used as a technical term of the Greek mystery religions, to refer to one initiated into mystic rites.

[16] "Present" is *paristēmi/paristanō*, "to cause to be present in any way." BDAG sees the usage in verses 22 and 28 as almost equivalent to "make, render." However, I think the idea is closer to its use as legal technical term, "bring before (a judge)" (BDAG 778, 1c, e).

"We proclaim him, admonishing and teaching everyone with all wisdom, so that we may present everyone perfect in Christ." (1:28)

Paul mentions three methods:

1. **"Proclaim"** (NIV, NRSV), **"preach"** (KJV) is *katangellō*, "to make known in public, with implication of broad dissemination, proclaim, announce."[17] This probably refers to his public ministry, heralding the Christ to those who hadn't heard the news.

2. **"Admonishing"** (NIV), **"warning"** (KJV, NRSV) is *noutheteō*, "to counsel about avoidance or cessation of an improper course of conduct, admonish, warn, instruct."[18] This method of perfecting the saints is more private – done either with a smaller group of believers or one-on-one.

    I believe in a positive approach to Christianity. In some traditions, people don't believe they've been to church unless the preacher tells them off in no uncertain terms. Frankly, that's not healthy. If all our children hear is admonishment and correction, they find it hard to receive the love we need to convey. So my advice is, let positive teaching and preaching be our main tools, with admonishing and warning to be used only as necessary – and sometimes they are certainly necessary, both at home and in the church.

3. **"Teaching"** is *didaskō*, "to provide instruction in a formal or informal setting."[19] This is the everyday instruction that would go on with individuals, families, and in the meetings of the believers. Notice the qualifier, "with all wisdom." Paul's teaching – and ours – must be carefully suited to the needs and spiritual level of those we instruct.

Finally, verse 29 details the work involved in bringing the saints to maturity in Christ. The phrases "labor, struggling" (NIV) "toil and struggle" (NRSV), "labor, striving" (KJV) translate a pair of words:

-   *Kopiaō* means to "to exert oneself physically, mentally, or spiritually, work hard, toil, strive, struggle."[20]

---

[17] *Katangellō*, BDAG 515, 1b.
[18] *Noutheteō*, BDAG 679.
[19] *Didaskō*, BDAG 223, 2b.
[20] *Kopiaō*, BDAG 558, 2.

- *Agōnizomai*, "to fight, struggle."[21] We'll examine the root of this verb in the next verse.

If you've never been a pastor or teacher, then you may not realize how much work goes into the process of building disciples and developing people's spiritual lives. Paul labored at it constantly, as must we.

Struggling in Prayer (2:1)

But the struggles Paul was talking about weren't primarily conflicts with immature deacons or even false teachers. His struggle was focused on prayer:

"I want you to know how much I am struggling for you and for those at Laodicea, and for all who have not met me personally." (2:1)

The word translated "struggling" (NIV, NRSV), "conflict" (KJV) is *agōn* from which we get our English word "agony." This Greek word was first used of the place where people assembled to watch athletic competition in the games. Later, it was used by extension to refer to "a struggle against opposition, struggle, fight."[22] Later in this letter Paul tells us about the founder of the church at Colossae, Epaphras:

"He is always wrestling (*agōnizomai*) in prayer for you...." (4:12)

Our normal view of prayer for others is a casual mention before God. But for Paul and Epaphras it was agonizing, long-term intercession on their behalf. Intercessors are the unsung heroes of the growth of the Christian church.

Q3. (Colossians 1:28-2:1) What is the purpose of Paul's labors according to verse 28? What does "perfect in Christ" mean? How does Paul accomplish this goal? In what way is he "struggling" for them?

http://www.joyfulheart.com/forums/index.php?showtopic=971

---

[21] *Agōnizomai*, BDAG 17, 2b.
[22] *Agōn*, BDAG 17, 2.

Complete Understanding (2:2-3)

Earlier we saw Paul's first formulation of the purpose of his ministry: "so that we may present everyone perfect in Christ" (1:28). Here he spells that out further:

> "[2] My purpose is that they may be encouraged in heart and united in love, so that they may have the full riches of complete understanding, in order that they may know the mystery of God, namely, Christ, [3] in whom are hidden all the treasures of wisdom and knowledge." (2:2-3)

This is a complex sentence. Let's take it apart so we can study it. Paul's purpose is:

> **That** they might be encouraged and find unity in love:
>> **So that** they might have complete understanding,
>>> **So that** they might know Christ fully.

It's like peeling an onion. Paul's ultimate goal is that the Colossian believers might know Christ in his fullness and understand enough to appreciate who Christ really is. For that to happen, Paul seeks two elements: encouragement and a stress on love for one another.

1. **"Encouraged"** (NIV, NRSV), "comforted" (KJV) is *parakaleō*, which here has the connotation, "to instill someone with courage or cheer, comfort, encourage, cheer up."[23]
2. **"United"** (NIV, NRSV) or "knit together" (KJV)[24] **in love**.

Why are these two elements so important to an in-depth understanding of Christ? We often think about understanding in conceptual, cognitive terms. But Paul is talking about more than a mental grasp of Christ. He is aware that for people to understand Christ at a deeper, spiritual level, they need to have hope (thus encouragement) as well as an experience of a loving Christian community ("knit together in love"). Thus it is extremely difficult for social hermits and lone-ranger Christians to really grasp Christ.

---

[23] *Parakaleō*, BDAG 765, 4.

[24] *Symbibazō* means figuratively, "unite, knit together" (BDAG 956, 1b). This is a compound verb, formed from *sun*, "with" + *bibazō*, "mount a female, copulate with her" (Thayer).

He can only be understood in the presence of love. With these can come complete[25] understanding.[26]

The goal is that the Colossians – and you and I today – know Christ fully. To the Jews, the "mystery" of Christ has been hidden from view. Paul's desire is full heart knowledge of Christ. "Know" (NIV), "knowledge" (NRSV), "acknowledgement" (KJV) is *epignōsis*, "knowledge, recognition,"[27] or as Thayer puts it, "precise and correct knowledge," emphasizing the idea of the preposition *epi-* in the compound word.[28]

When Paul reaches a mention of Christ in this letter, he can't resist an opportunity to display Christ's uniqueness and supremacy (to counteract the false teachers in Colossae):

> "... The mystery of God, namely, Christ, in whom are hidden all the treasures of wisdom and knowledge." (2:2b-3)

How is Christ a treasure-box or treasure-house[29] in which are hidden[30] God's profound wisdom (*sophia*) and knowledge (*gnōsis*)? Some of the mystery religions of Paul's day emphasized secret knowledge (*gnōsis*), a trend that led in the following century to the full-blown Gnostic movement. Paul is saying that wisdom and knowledge are not some special privilege passed secretly to the elite. They are found in Christ himself and Christ alone. And to know him intimately and fully – the privilege of all Christian believers – is to possess the full treasure-house of God's wisdom and knowledge.

---

[25] "Complete" (NIV), "assured" (NRSV), "assurance" (KJV) is *plērophoria*, "state of complete certainty, full assurance, certainty" (BDAG 827).

[26] "Understanding" is *synesis*, "the faculty of comprehension, intelligence, acuteness, shrewdness," in the religio-ethical realm "understanding" (BDAG 970, 1b).

[27] *Epignōsis*, BDAG 369.

[28] *Epignōsis* is a compound word formed from *epi-* "accumulation, increase, addition" + *gnōsis*, "knowledge. Rudolf Bultmann notes that in some passages, "the compound *epignōsis* can take on almost a technical sense for conversion to Christianity" (*Gnōsis, ktl.*, TDNT 1:689–719)."

[29] "Treasures" is *thēsauros*, (from which we get the English word "thesaurus"), "a place where something is kept for safekeeping, repository," then, "that which is stored up, treasure" (BDAG 456, 2bγ).

[30] "Hidden" (NIV, NRSV), "hid" (KJV) is *apokryphos*, adjective, "hidden" (BDAG 114).

Q4. (Colossians 2:2-3) In what sense are "all the treasures of wisdom and knowledge" hidden in Christ? What does that mean?

http://www.joyfulheart.com/forums/index.php?showtopic=972

Let No One Deceive You (2:4-5)

"[4] I tell you this so that no one may deceive you by fine-sounding arguments. [5] For though I am absent from you in body, I am present with you in spirit and delight to see how orderly you are and how firm your faith in Christ is." (2:4-5)

"I tell you this," says Paul. He is referring, of course, to the sufficiency and completeness of Christ, who is for the Colossian believers their "hope of glory" (1:27). They don't need what is being offered by the mystical Jewish teachers and all their "fine-sounding arguments."[31] These false teachers are seeking to deceive[32] them, pure and simple.

After warning them of the deceit, he encourages them. I am with you in spirit, Paul says. And I delight to see how well you are doing in Christ. Keep it up.[33]

And so Paul closes this portion of his letter. He begins with assurance of his delight in their faith and love. Then he points to Christ's supremacy over any other religion or philosophy. In this lesson's passage he has assured them of Paul's own ministry that is supporting them through prayer. Now, just before he tackles some of the false teachers' errors head on, he offers them words of encouragement.

Dear friends, don't discount the value of your labor in the Lord. The years you have served Christ, perhaps spent in teaching Sunday school children, has helped establish their hearts in Christ. You, along with the Apostle Paul, have partnered with others to present them perfect in Christ. It is not wasted effort!

---

[31] "Fine-sounding arguments" (NIV), "plausible arguments" (NRSV), "enticing words" (KJV) is *pithanologia*, "persuasive speech, art of persuasion," here, "by specious arguments" (BDAG 812).

[32] "Deceive" (NIV, NRSV), "beguile" (KJV) is *paralogizomai*, "deceive, delude," from *para-*, "violation, neglect, aberration" + *logizomai*, "reckon, calculate." (BDAG 768).

[33] Paul uses two words to describe the Colossians' state. First, "orderly" (NIV), "morale" (NRSV), "order" (KJV), is *taxis*, "a state of good order, order, proper procedure" (BDAG 989, 2). Then "firm/firmness" (NIV, NRSV), "steadfastness" (KJV), *stereōma*, "state or condition of firm commitment, firmness, steadfastness." (BDAG 943, 2).

And the sufferings you have experienced in ministry have made you a sharer in the sufferings of Christ himself! Your ministry in prayer, too, will bear fruit. Continue on, dear friends, in your faithful ministry for Christ. One of my favorite verses encourages me when I am discouraged:

> "Therefore, my beloved brethren, be steadfast, immovable, always abounding in the work of the Lord, knowing that in the Lord your labor is not in vain." (1 Corinthians 15:58)

Prayer

Father, I thank you for your dear people who serve you faithfully. Encourage them, help them, and send forth more laborers into your harvest as some of the harvesters take their long-awaited rest. In Jesus' name, I pray. Amen.

, NIVs

> "To them God has chosen to make known among the Gentiles the glorious riches of this mystery, which is Christ in you, the hope of glory." (Colossians 1:27, NIV)

> " We proclaim him, admonishing and teaching everyone with all wisdom, so that we may present everyone perfect in Christ." (Colossians 1:28, NIV)

> "... Christ, in whom are hidden all the treasures of wisdom and knowledge." (Colossians 2:2b-3, NIV)

5. Freedom from Legalism (Colossians 2:6-23)

Paul is about to confront head on the false teaching that has tempted the Colossians to revert to a speculative and mystical form of Judaism. But first he reminds them of the beauty of the gospel which they had first received in the early days of the church, a few years before. Paul had described this early in the letter.

We begin this lesson with a "therefore" (NRSV, KJV) or "so then" (NIV)[1] based on what Paul has said so far:

James J. Tissot, "False Witnesses" (1896-1903), watercolor, Brooklyn Museum, New York

- Paul's thanksgiving for their faith and love,

- Christ's preeminence over any created being, and

- Paul's sacrificial ministry to bring the gospel to their area....

Characteristics of our Relationship with Christ (2:6-7)

"[6] **So then**, just as you received[2] Christ Jesus as Lord, continue to live in him, [7] rooted and built up in him, strengthened in the faith as you were taught, and overflowing with thankfulness." (2:6-7)

Paul appeals to their strong past in Christ, as a way to hold them steady for the present and future. Christ has been your Lord, he says. You "live" (NIV) or "walk" (NRSV, KJV) in him, that is, conduct your life in Christ's way and in his path.[3]

---

[1] "So then" (NIV), "therefore" (NRSV, KJV) is *oun*, "inferential, denoting that what it introduces is the result of or an inference from what precedes, 'so, therefore, consequently, accordingly, then'" (BDAG 737, 1b).

[2] "Received" is *paralambanō*, "to gain control of or receive jurisdiction over, take over, receive," here, of a mental or spiritual heritage, 'accept Christ Jesus,' that is, the proclamation of him as Lord" (BDAG 768, 2bγ).

Paul highlights four characteristics of their walk or journey with Christ as their Lord. Each of the images depict what it's like to become mature in Christ.

1. **Rooted in Christ**. They were once tender transplants, but now they have taken firm root, figuratively, they have been "put on a firm foundation, fix firmly."[4]

2. **Built up in Christ**. Paul uses a word from the construction trades to describe their growth: "to engage in a building process of personal and corporate development, edify, build up, build on."[5]

3. **Strengthened in faith**. The word comes from the root *basis*, "foot" (from which we get our word "basis"). It means "to make a person firm in commitment, establish, strengthen,"[6] to make them firm upon their foundation.

4. **Overflowing with thankfulness**. The imagery here is having abundance, being rich. Here the idea is to "be outstanding, be prominent, excel" in thankfulness.[7]

Deceptive Philosophy (2:8)

You've come a long way, Paul is saying. Don't let the wonderful place you have be replaced with a kind of bondage.

"[8] See to it that no one takes you captive through hollow and deceptive philosophy, which depends on human tradition and the basic principles of this world rather than on Christ." (2:8)

The false teachers' motives are not benign, Paul warns. They want to "take you captive." The word is *sylagōgeō*, "to gain control of by carrying off as booty, make captive of, rob."[8] The imagery is of carrying someone away from the truth into the slavery of error. KJV uses "to spoil" in the archaic sense of "to despoil." The false teachers want to take from you the treasure that you have in Christ.

---

[3] "Continue to live" (NIV), "live your lives" (NRSV), "walk" (KJV) is the present imperative of *peripateō*, "walk," figuratively, "to conduct one's life, comport oneself, behave, live as habit of conduct" (BDAG 803, 2aδ).

[4] *Rhizoō*, BDAG 906. We get our botanical word "rhizome" from this Greek word stem.

[5] *Epoikodomeō*, BDAG 387, 2.

[6] *Bebaioō*, BDAG 172, 2.

[7] *Perisseuō*, BDAG 805, 2bβ.

[8] *Sylagōgeō*, BDAG 955.

But the replacement they offer isn't what they claim. Rather, it is hollow, empty.[9] They make it look grand, but there is no substance. What they offer is nothing compared to what you already have. What's more, their approach is deceptive.[10] They're not telling the truth.

Paul characterizes the false teachers' doctrine as "philosophy" is *philosophia*, literally *philos*, "love" + *sophia*, "wisdom." The Greek word goes back to the sixth century BC, of those who strive for knowledge, especially worthwhile knowledge of a comprehensive nature. Various Greek philosophical schools arose – Sophists, followers of Plato, Aristotle, and Epicurus, Stoicism, and others. Paul's letters sometimes use terminology that arose in philosophical schools. But here Paul uses "philosophy" with a negative connotation to refer to the belief system of the false teachers in Colossae, who made claims about their weighty authority. Paul disparages them by calling their philosophy "hollow and deceptive," that is, both empty and false.[11]

The pillars that uphold the false teachers' philosophy are not of Christ. They are not Messianic truths, Paul warns. Rather, the hidden supports for their doctrine are two-fold:

1. **Tradition,**[12] concepts and accepted truths that have been passed on from one generation to another – but are nevertheless devoid of truth.

2. **Elemental spirits** (NRSV). This is a difficult word to translate into our culture and worldview. *Stoicheion* refers to the "basic components of something, elements." Here it may refer to "transcendent powers that are in control over events in this world, elements, elemental spirits."[13] Paul is probably alluding to evil spirits who are under the control of the "god of this world" (2 Corinthians 4:4), the spirits who are behind worldly philosophies.[14]

---

[9] "Hollow" (NIV), "empty" (NRSV), "vain" (KJV) is *kenos*, "pertaining to being devoid of intellectual, moral, or spiritual value, empty," of things, "without content, without any basis, without truth, without power" (BDAG 539, 2a).

[10] "Deceptive" (NIV), "deceit" (KJV) is *apatē*, "deception, deceitfulness" (BDAG 99, 1).

[11] See Otto Michel, *philosophia, philosophos*, TDNT 9:172-188.

[12] "Tradition" is *paradosis*, "the content of instruction that has been handed down, tradition" (BDAG 763, 2).

[13] *Stoicheion*, BDAG 946, 2. It is translated, "basic principles" (NIV), "elemental spirits" (NRSV), "rudiments" (KJV).

[14] Moo, *Colossians*, pp. 187-192 for a careful discussion.

What the false teachers offer sounds good, but it is hollow, deceptive, and part of the "same old, same old" combination of tradition and false beliefs that the enemy has been propagating for millennia. See it for what it is, says Paul.

Q1. (Colossians 2:8) Philosophy refers to a prevailing belief system. How can a belief system be empty and false? Have you ever personally experienced being captivated by a belief system only to find it deceptive and hollow?
http://www.joyfulheart.com/forums/index.php?showtopic=973

The Fullness of Deity in Bodily Form (2:9-10)

Contrast the empty philosophy that the false teachers offer with who Christ is, says Paul. There is no comparison!

"⁹ For in Christ all the fullness of the Deity lives in bodily form, ¹⁰ and you have been given fullness in Christ, who is the head over every power and authority." (2:9-10)

Wow! Say these two verses over to yourself a few times to grasp their breadth and import. The false teachers are offering fulfillment and fullness by laying hold of something beyond Christ the Messiah. But there is nothing and no one closer to God, no experience fuller, than knowing him and walking with him.

Let's spend a few minutes examining the words in these two key verses.

First, it says that "in Christ all the fullness of the Deity lives in bodily form." The word "lives" (NIV) or "dwells" (NRSV, cf.KJV) is *katoikeō*, "to live in a locality for any length of time, live, dwell, reside, settle (down)."[15] In ancient Greek it refers to long-time residence, "settle in, colonize."[16] In the New Testament the word is used in a literal, geographical sense to refer to people "living in" Jerusalem, of Abraham's family "living in" Haran, of Jews "living in" Damascus.[17] But the word has a special sense to refer to God's Spirit inhabiting a human being:

---

[15] *Katoikeō*, BDAG 534, 1b.
[16] *Katoikeō*, Liddell-Scott.
[17] Luke 13:4; Acts 7:2; 9:22, for example.

"That Christ may **dwell** in your hearts by faith." (Ephesians 3:17)

"... The Spirit he **caused to live**[18] in us." (James 4:5)

"And in him you too are being built together to become a **dwelling**[19] in which God lives by his Spirit." (Ephesians 2:22)

The word is used twice in Colossians of Christ himself.

"For God was pleased to have all his fullness **dwell** in him." (1:19)

"For in Christ all the fullness of the Deity **lives** in bodily form." (2:9)

God dwells in his Son, the Messiah, the Christ. He does not dwell in us in the same degree as he dwells in his Son. We are merely creatures, fallen from God's perfect creation, who are being gradually restored by the Spirit to our full glory (2 Corinthians 3:18; 4:16-17). But Christ is not a created being, but the Creator himself, for "all things were created by him and for him" (1:16). Jesus is "one" with the Father (John 1:30), glorified with the Father before all creation (John 17:5). He is God in the flesh (John 1:14), the "only begotten God" (John 1:18, NASB).

God in the Flesh

Because Jesus himself is God, God dwells in him completely, fully, in the flesh.

"For in Christ all the fullness of the Deity lives in bodily form." (2:9)

The nature of this indwelling is spelled out in several Greek words:

1. Quality of Christ's Deity

"Deity" (NIV, NRSV) or "Godhead" (KJV) in 2:9 is *theotēs*, a word which occurs only here in the New Testament. It means, "the state of being god, divine character/nature, deity, divinity." The King James' translation "Godhead" over-translates the word, since the concept of "head" or "headship" isn't included in the Greek meaning of the word.[20] However, this word *theotēs*, "deity," is to be distinguished from *theiotēs*, "divinity," "an attribute which might conceivably be possessed by a being of lesser standing than God himself."[21]

---

[18] Causative verb, *katoikizō*, "cause to dwell, establish, settle" (BDAG 535).

[19] The noun form, *katoikētērion*, "dwelling place" (BDAG 534).

[20] *Theotēs*, BDAG 452. "Divinity, divine nature" (Liddell-Scott).

[21] Wright, *Colossians*, pp. 107-108.

2. Degree of Christ's Deity

"Fullness" is *plērōma*, which we saw in 1:19, "sum total, fullness, even (super) abundance."[22] So the Divinity doesn't dwell in Jesus *partly*, or in *some* measure, like he does in us. In Christ, God dwells *completely*, expressed by the phrase "**all the fullness** of the Deity."[23]

3. Expression of Christ's Deity

The manner of dwelling is described as: "in bodily form" (NIV), "bodily" (NRSV, KJV). This is the adverb *sōmatikōs*, "bodily, corporeally," as opposed to noncorporaelly, from *sōma*, "body."[24] Paul is talking about the incarnation, which means literally, "in-fleshment" (from *in* + *carne*, "flesh, meat"). Jesus of Nazareth is God in the flesh, deity in bodily form.

4. Authority of Christ's Deity

Verse 10 talks about the authority of Christ's deity.

"... Christ, who is the **head over** every power and authority." (2:10)

Earlier in his letter, Paul has explained that Christ is "head" over the church. But his headship extends over everything he has created – including the evil spiritual powers that are opponents of the Church that we discussed previously. In Paul's letter to the Ephesians -- penned about the same time as Colossians and with many similar themes -- Paul says:

"[God] seated him at his right hand in the heavenly realms, far above all rule and authority, power and dominion, and every title that can be given, not only in the present age but also in the one to come. [22] And God placed all things under his feet and appointed him to be **head over everything** for the church...." (Ephesians 2:20-22)

---

[22] *Plērōma*, BDAG 829, 3b.

[23] A century after Colossians was written, the term *plērōma* had come to be a Gnostic technical term for various lesser supernatural beings emanating from God, as a kind of second-level intermediary, but we can't assume that the word had this meaning in Paul's day.

[24] *Sōmatikōs*, BDAG 984. G.B. Caird (*Paul's Letters from Prison (Ephesians, Philippians, Colossians, Philemon) in the Revised Standard Version: Introduction and Commentary* (Oxford, 1976), pp. 191-192) argues that "in bodily form" can also mean "actually" or "in solid reality," citing 2:17 (shadow vs. reality) as a parallel. But Paul's point here is to underscore the incarnation, God in the flesh.

In these verses *kephalē*, "head," is used to denote superior rank of a being of high status over another.[25] The Colossians have nothing to fear from spiritual powers, nor does a mystical Judaism have anything over Christianity, for Christ has authority over all powers in heaven and on earth.

Complete in Him! (2:10)

This powerful passage concludes with Paul's assurance to the Colossians about their standing in Christ. See how various versions translate it:

"And you have been given fullness in Christ...." (NIV)
"And you have come to fullness in him...." (NRSV)
"And in Him you have been made complete...." (NASB)
"And ye are complete in him...." (KJV)

The verb is *plēroō*, "to make full, full(fill)," used of persons, "fill" with powers, qualities, etc.[26]

What a wonderful truth – we are made complete and find our fulfillment in Christ and in him alone. We don't need to add anything more. In *him* we are completed! You can rest in the sufficiency of Christ's love and redemption. Relax and enjoy him. You are complete in him!

If Paul's letter to the Colossians has a center, a central thesis, it is here! The false teachers are trying to deceive members of this young church that they need something more. Paul's answer? A resounding, "No!" You are complete in Christ!

I know I've spent some time on these two verses, but the truth is so important and life-changing that it is crucial that we grasp it.

Q2. (Colossians 2:9-10) What does verse 9 teach about Christ's full divinity? In what sense are we "complete" or "come to fullness" in Christ? What does this mean? Why do we sometimes fail to understand this fullness?
http://www.joyfulheart.com/forums/index.php?showtopic=974

---

[25] *Kephalē*, BDAG 542, 2a.
[26] *Plēroō*, BDAG 828, 1b.

Spiritual Circumcision (2:11-12)

Now Paul brings up the subject of circumcision, probably because the Jewish false teachers were telling the Gentile Christians that they needed to be circumcised in order to be truly saved. Not so, says Paul.

> "[11] In him you were also circumcised,[27] in the putting off[28] of the sinful nature, not with a circumcision done by the hands of men but with the circumcision done by Christ, [12] having been buried with[29] him in baptism and raised with[30] him through your faith in the power[31] of God, who raised him from the dead." (2:11-12)

Verses 11 and 12 are a difficult sentence to understand, so I've broken it down logically. You don't need anything more, says Paul, because...

1. In Christ your hearts were **purified** (symbolized by circumcision):

    o   This circumcision was not in human flesh, but spiritual, in that your sinful nature (literally, *sarx*, "flesh") was dethroned.

    o   This was not some human ritual like circumcision, but a supernatural work done by Christ.

2. AND you were **united** with Christ (symbolized by baptism):

    o   Baptism is a symbol of both spiritual union with Christ in his death and in his resurrection.

We could spend more time here, but the images are confusing to the twenty-first century mind, so we'll move on.[32]

---

[27] *Peritemnō*, "to cut off the foreskin of the male genital organ, circumcise," figurative. (BDAG 807, bα). *Peritomē*, "circumcision." (BDAG 807, 1c).

[28] "Putting off" is *apekdysis*, "removal, stripping off of clothes" (BDAG 100).

[29] "Buried" is *synthaptō*, "bury (together) with" (BDAG 971).

[30] "Raised with" *synegeirō*, originally, "to cause to emerge with from an inactive state, awaken with," then figuratively, "to raise up with from death, physical or spiritual, raise with" (BDAG 967, 2b). It is used in this sense in Colossians 2:12; 3:1 and Ephesians 2:6.

[31] "Power" (NIV, NRSV), "operation" (KJV) is *energeia*, "the state or quality of being active, working, operation, action" (BDAG 335).

[32] Note that this is the only time in the Bible that circumcision (the rite of inclusion in the Old Covenant) and baptism (the rite of inclusion in the New Covenant) appear together. Sometimes those who teach infant baptism use this verse to support their position, but in doing so they miss Paul's intention. This passage has nothing to do with infant baptism, either for or against.

Made Alive in Christ (2:13-14)

As we mine verses 13 and 14 we find a rich vein of gold.

"[13] When you were dead in your sins and in the uncircumcision of your sinful nature, God made you alive with Christ. He forgave us all our sins, [14] having canceled the written code, with its regulations, that was against us and that stood opposed to us; he took it away, nailing it to the cross." (2:13-14)

Paul uses three figures to describe our state before our salvation:

1. Spiritually dead.

2. Uncircumcised, that is unpurified in the "flesh" (*sarx*).[33]

3. Unforgiven, that is, "in your sins."

He uses three figures to describe the results of Christ's salvation:

1. Made spiritually alive.[34]

2. Forgiven[35] of *all* our sins.[36]

3. Freed from the law.

The Written Code is Cancelled (2:14)

This last act of salvation, being freed from the law, needs further explanation. Look carefully at verse 14 again:

"... Having canceled the written code, with its regulations, that was against us and that stood opposed to us; he took it away, nailing it to the cross." (2:14)

The question here is what is the Christian's relationship to the Mosaic law and its requirements. Jesus had said clearly in the Sermon on the Mount:

"Do not think that I have come to abolish the Law or the Prophets; I have not come to abolish them but to **fulfill**[37] them. I tell you the truth, until heaven and earth

---

[33] Here Paul is making a play on words. Circumcision is performed on human tissue, but by "flesh" here he is referring to the unregenerate human nature that is prone to sin and in rebellion against God.

[34] "Made alive (together) with" (NIV, NRSV), "quickened together with" (KJV) is *syzōopoieō*, "make alive together with someone," also at Ephesians 2:5 (BDAG 954).

[35] "Forgave" (NIV, NRSV), "having forgiven" (KJV) is *charizomai*, basically, "to give freely as a favor, give graciously," here, "to show oneself gracious by forgiving wrongdoing, forgive, pardon" (BDAG 107, 3). The word is also used in 3:13.

[36] "Sins" (NIV), "trespasses" (NRSV, KJV) is *paraptōma*, "a violation of moral standards, offense, wrongdoing, sin" (BDAG 770, bγ).

disappear, not the smallest letter, not the least stroke of a pen, will by any means disappear from the Law until everything is **accomplished**."[38] (Matthew 5:17-18)

By "accomplished," Jesus seems to be referring to all the events that must take place that have been prophesied for the Messiah, especially his death in our place, his burial, and his resurrection. "Nailing[39] it to the cross" suggests that it has been fulfilled on the cross.

Two words describe the removal of the law.

1. **"Cancelled"** (NIV), **"erasing"** (NRSV), **"blotting out"** (KJV) is *exaleiphō*. The primary meaning is, "to cause to disappear by wiping." Here it has the more specific meaning, "to remove so as to leave no trace, remove, destroy, obliterate."[40] Elsewhere we read that the law has been annulled because it has become weak, useless, and obsolete (Hebrews 7:18; 8:13). A number of times the scripture talks about blotting out sins and transgressions (Psalms 51:1, 9; Isaiah 43:25; Acts 3:19), but here the written code[41] that stood against us[42] – the Mosaic law itself is erased – a strong word.

2. **"Took away"** (NIV), **"set aside"** (NRSV), is rendered quite literally by the KJV as "took out of the way." "Way" is *mesos* , "midst, from among." The verb is *airō*. The word originally meant, "lift up, take up, pick up." But here, it means, "to take away, remove, or seize control" without suggestion of lifting up. In the case of "a bond, note, certificate of indebtedness, "destroy."[43]

---

[37] "Fulfill" is *plēroō*, "to complete, fulfill," which we saw earlier in this lesson.

[38] "Accomplished" (NIV, NRSV) or "fulfilled" (KJV) at the end of verse 18 is *ginomai*, "happen." It is probably used in the sense here, "to occur as process or result, happen, turn out, take place" (BDAG 197, 4a).

[39] "Nailing" is *prosēloō*, "to nail (fast)" (BDAG 880).

[40] *Exaleiphō*, BDAG 344, 2.

[41] The terms translated "written code" (NIV), "handwriting of ordinances" (KJV), "the record ... with its legal demands" (NRSV), actually comprise two words: (1) *cheirographon*, "a hand-written document," specifically, "a certificate of indebtedness, account, record of debts." E. Lohse calls it, "A document is written in one's own hand as a proof of obligation, such as, a note of indebtedness. The meaning in Colossians 2:14, then, is a 'promissory note.'" (E. Lohse, *cheir, ktl.*, TDNT 9:424-437). (2) The second word is *dogma*, the source of our English word "dogma," which means, "something that is taught as an established tenet or statement of belief." Here, however, it has something of its original usage, "a formal statement concerning rules or regulations that are to be observed, ordinance, decision, command" (BDAG 254, 1a).

[42] "Against" is the preposition *kata*, "down upon, toward, against someone or something," here, in a hostile sense, "against" (BDAG 518, 2bβ). "Stood opposed" (NIV), "stood against" (NRSV), "contrary to" (KJV) is the adjective *hypenantios*, "opposed, contrary, hostile." (BDAG 103).

[43] *Airō*, BDAG 29, 3.

Did Jesus substitute a soft, squishy law of love for the hard, unrelenting demands of the Mosaic Law? No! He fulfilled the Mosaic Law on our behalf, drinking its bitter cup down to the very dregs on the cross. This is no cheap grace. The demands of the law have been fulfilled totally in Christ's death. Now that Messiah has come and his Spirit has been poured out, the Law is no longer our guide; the Holy Spirit is. The Old Covenant's role is over in this age of the New Covenant, made possible by the shedding of Christ's blood. It is finished!

Disarming the Evil Spiritual Powers (2:15)

Now we read a fascinating statement:

> "And having disarmed the powers and authorities, he made a public spectacle of them, triumphing over them by the cross." (2:15)

"Disarmed" (NIV, NRSV), "spoiled" (KJV) is *apekdyomai*, an emphatic word. A related word, *apodyō/ynō* was used by Homer (especially in the *Illiad*) of stripping armor from the slain.[44] "Triumphing" is *thriambeuō*, "lead in a triumphal procession."[45] The image is of a public[46] triumphal parade following a decisive military victory, with the disgraced[47] and defeated foe marching behind the victor, as alluded to in Ephesians 4:8 (quoting Psalm 68:18).

The final clause is a little hard to translate accurately.

> "... triumphing over them by the cross." (NIV)

> "... triumphing over them in it." (NRSV, KJV)

---

[44] *Apodyō/ynō*, Liddell-Scott. *Ekdyō/ynō* was also used for "to strip." Paul combines the prepositions *apo-*, "separation, liberation, cessation, departure" + *ek-*, "emission, removal, separation" also "equivalent to 'utterly, entirely,' " (Thayer) for "an expression of complete removal." (Robertson, *Word Pictures*). *Dynō*, "to put on, don" (Georg Autenrieth. *A Homeric Dictionary for Schools and Colleges* (New York. Harper and Brothers, 1891)), but our word "does not mean 'to divest oneself of,' but 'to disarm' (opposite of *dýō*, 'to arm oneself')" (Albrecht Oepke, TDNT 2:318-321). Later in Colossians 3:9, *apekdyomai* means to "take off, strip off," of clothes (BDAG 100, 1 and 2). But in 2:15 the image is a decisive military triumph.

[45] The image is either of a parade of conquered enemies or as a general does leading his army (Liddell-Scott). Here the word should probably be translated "triumph over" (or perhaps "expose to shame," but that isn't the main thrust of the word) (BDAG 459, 4 and 5). The word "is derived from *thriambos*, a hymn sung in festal procession and is kin to the Latin *triumphus* (our 'triumph'), a triumphal procession of victorious Roman generals" (Robertson, *Word Pictures*).

[46] "Public" (NIV, NRSV), "openly" (KJV) is *en parrēsia*, "openness to the public, in public, publicly" (BDAG 783, 2).

[47] "Made a spectacle" (NIV), "made an example" (NRSV), "made a shew" (KJV) is *deigmatizō*, "expose, make an example of, disgrace someone" (BDAG 214).

The Greek text contains a masculine pronoun "it" or "him," not "cross," which the NIV supplies to bring out the meaning better. There are two possible referents for the pronoun:

- "The cross" (verse 14)

- "Christ" (verse 13)

There's no way to be absolutely sure which Paul meant, nor does it matter greatly. "Cross" is the closer referent, while the entire sentence is about Christ's work.

The real question, of course, is: In what sense did Christ disarm these evil powers? How complete was the victory? The letter to the Colossians doesn't answer this question. We have a few passages in the New Testament that may shed some light on this, however.

- **Binding the strong man.** Jesus relates a parable that points to his overpowering Satan and taking his goods (Matthew 12:29; Luke 11:22).

- **Satan falling from heaven.** Jesus alludes to Satan's fall from heaven when the 70 report their ability to cast out demons, but the time frame isn't specified (Luke 10:18).

- **Prince of the world driven out** seems to be tied to Jesus' death (John 12:31).

- **War in heaven** is a vision in Revelation, where Satan is thrown out of heaven when he tries to destroy the Messiah and the church (Revelation 12).

- **Satan is bound** for 1,000 years, then released, fights the final war against the Messiah, and is thrown into the lake of fire (Revelation 20).

If Christ disarmed and conquered the principalities and powers on the cross, why do we still have to fight them (Ephesians 6:10-18)? We don't know fully. The decisive battle was won on the cross. Satan was weakened and the church given power over him, but Satan has not been fully destroyed. This is part of the "now and in the future" nature of the Kingdom of God. The Kingdom is here now, but will come in its fullness -- and Satan will be defeated completely and utterly -- after Christ returns.

Q3. (Colossians 2:13-15) How did forgiveness free us from the Law? What is the significance of nailing the Law to the cross? What does this symbolize? How did the cross bring triumph over evil spiritual forces?
http://www.joyfulheart.com/forums/index.php?showtopic=975

Discarding the Shadow for the Reality (2:16-17)

We've focused most of our time on what Paul says about who Christ is and what he has done in us and for us. But now Paul gets specific about some of the elements of false teaching with which the mystical Jewish sect in Colossae was tempting the young church:

> "16 Therefore do not let anyone judge you by what you eat or drink, or with regard to a religious festival, a New Moon celebration or a Sabbath day. 17 These are a shadow of the things that were to come; the reality, however, is found in Christ." (2:16-17)

In verse 16 Paul mentions four elements of Judaism by which the false teachers were putting down and criticizing the church:

1. **Food regulations**. Since the time of Moses, the Jews had observed complex rules concerning clean and unclean animals, outlined in Leviticus 11, and then expanded upon and interpreted by rabbis over the centuries. The Council of Jerusalem decided not to require Gentile Christians to observe Jewish food laws (Acts 15:1-21; Romans 14:14; 1 Timothy 4:3-5; Matthew 15:11).

2. **Religious festivals**,[48] probably including Passover, Pentecost, etc. Early Jewish-Christians (and Paul, on occasion; Acts 20:11) observed these festivals, but they were not part of the life of the Gentile church (Galatians 4:10).

3. **New Moon** celebrations[49] were common in Judaism (Numbers 10:10; 28:11; Nehemiah 10:33; Psalm 81:3; Isaiah 1:13).

---

[48] "Religious festival" (NIV), "festivals" (NRSV), "holyday" (KJV) is *heortē*, " a day or series of days marked by a periodic celebration or observance, festival, celebration" (BDAG 355).

4. **Sabbath day.**[50] Though the Sabbath day was enjoined in the Ten Commandments, Gentile Christians celebrated the first day of the week (John 20:19; 20:26; Acts 20:7; 1 Corinthians 16:2), the day on which Christ had risen, which they called the Lord's Day (Revelation 1:10).

Paul sees these Jewish practices as intended to teach and prepare God's people for the reality that was to come when the Messiah appeared.

"These are a shadow of the things that were to come; the reality, however, is found in Christ." (2:17)

We see also this language of shadow and reality (or substance)[51] in relation to Judaism and Christ in the Book of Hebrews (Hebrews 8:5; 10:1). This may sound a bit like Plato's idealism, his allegory of the cave, in which shadows projected on a wall appear to be real, while they are only shadows of the actual people,[52] but clearly Paul's root ideas are based in the Old Testament.

Mystical Jewish Practices (2:16-18)

So far, Paul has explained why Gentile followers of the Messiah have no reason to adopt Jewish practices. Now he attacks the specific practices of the mystical Jewish sect around Colossae that is trying to entice the Christian believers.

"Do not let anyone who delights[53] in false humility and the worship of angels disqualify you for the prize. Such a person goes into great detail about what he has seen, and his unspiritual mind puffs him up with idle notions." (2:18)

Just like the writer of Hebrews, Paul sees returning to Judaism of any sort a step backward, and a denial of the Messiah. The phrase "disqualify for the prize" (NIV), "disqualify" (NRSV), "beguile of your reward" (KJV) is *katabrabeuō*, "'decide against' (as

---

[49] "New Moon" is *neomēnia*, "new moon, first of the month, often celebrated as a festival by Jews and Gentiles (BDAG 669).

[50] "Sabbath Day" (NIV), "sabbath days" (KJV) is *sabbaton*, the seventh day of the week in Israel's calendar, marked by rest from work and by special religious ceremonies, sabbath." Here it is in the plural -- "sabbaths" (BDAG 910, 1bβ).

[51] "Reality" (NIV), "substance" (NRSV), "body" (KJV) is *sōma*, "body," here, "substantive reality, the thing itself, the reality," in imagery of a body that casts a shadow, in contrast to *skia*, "shadow" (BDAG 984, 4).

[52] Plato, *Republic*, book 7, 514A, 520A

[53] "Delights" (NIV), "insisting" (NRSV), "voluntary" (KJV) is *thelō*, "desire, wish to have, want." It probably means "to take pleasure in, like" (as in the NIV), but could have the connotation, "to have an opinion, maintain contrary to the true state of affairs" (as in the NRSV's "insist") (BDAG 448, 3b).

umpire), and so rob of a prize, condemn," from *kata-*, "against" + *brabeuō*, "to be an umpire in a contest."[54]

Verse 18 mentions three characteristics of this sect:

- **False humility**. The false teachers put on a guise of humility (perhaps including ascetic practices such as fasting[55]), but in fact they were full of pride[56] about their supposed spiritual prowess. They projected an aura of spirituality, but in fact were "unspiritual."[57]

- **Worship[58] of angels**. Other sources attest to the worship of angels in Phrygia and Pisidia in the early centuries of the Christian era.[59] Angel worship wasn't standard in Judaism as a whole, but probably was present in Colossae through syncretism with local religious beliefs, perhaps in a belief that angels would protect them from evil.[60]

- **Visions** (NRSV) or "what is seen" (NIV)[61] were a third characteristic of the local brand of mystical Judaism. The false teachers would go into great detail[62] about these visions.

Connection with the Head (2:19)

Paul warns the Colossians about such false teachers:

> "He has lost connection with the Head, from whom the whole body, supported and held together by its ligaments and sinews, grows as God causes it to grow." (2:19)

---

[54] *Katabrabeuō*, BDAG 515.

[55] Moo, *Colossians*, p. 226. The Greek word is "self-abasement (NRSV).

[56] "Puff up" is *physioō*, literally, "to blow up, inflate" (from *physa*, "pair of bellows"), figurative, "to cause to have an exaggerated self-conception, puff up, make proud" (BDAG 106).

[57] "Unspiritual" (NIV), "human way of thinking" (NRSV), "fleshly" (KJV) is *sarx*.

[58] "Worship/worshipping" is *thrēskeia*, "'expression of devotion to transcendent beings, especially as it expresses itself in cultic rites, worship,' the being who is worshiped is given in the objective genitive" (BDAG 459).

[59] Ramsay, CB I/2 p. 541 no. 404 and p. 741 no. 678 testify to the worship of angels in Phrygia. The Council of Laodicea, Can. 35 rejects it; Theodoret III 490 [on Col 2:16] deplores its tenacious survival in Phrygia and Pisidia (*thrēskeia*, BDAG 459).

[60] Moo, *Colossians*, p. 227, citing Clinton Arnold, *The Colossian Syncretism* (WUNT 77; Tübigen: Mohr Siebeck, 1995), pp. 61-101.

[61] *Horaō*, "to see." (BDAG 726, 1c).

[62] "Goes into great detail" (NIV), "dwelling on " (NRSV), "intruding into" (KJV) is *embateuō*, "investigate closely, enter into a subject to investigate it closely, go into detail" (BDAG 322, 3).

The NIV's "lost connection" is perhaps too strong, suggesting that the false teachers had once held to Christ. Closer to the Greek are "not holding fast" (NRSV) and "not holding" (KJV).[63]

Christ is the one who makes sense out of faith. So many churches are just religious shells. They have their ritual and their rites, based solidly on their traditions. But they have lost an intimate connection to him who gives life. Even right doctrine (in contrast to the false teachers in Colossae) can't substitute for a close, personal connection to the Head. All growth comes by means of nourishment from him, and him only.[64]

The Emptiness of Human Regulations (2:20-23)

In place of a relationship to Christ, the false teachers had imposed all sorts of rules. Paul asks his readers:

> "[20] Since you died with Christ to the basic principles[65] of this world, why, as though you still belonged to it, do you submit to its rules:[66] [21] 'Do not handle! Do not taste! Do not touch!'? [22] These are all destined to perish[67] with use, because they are based on human commands and teachings. [23] Such regulations indeed have an appearance[68] of wisdom, with their self-imposed worship, their false humility and their harsh treatment of the body, but they lack any value in restraining sensual indulgence." (2:20-23)

Paul makes three points in these verses:

---

[63] "Not" plus the verb, *krateō*, "to adhere strongly to, hold" ... of commitment to someone or something "hold fast (to)" (BDAG 565, 6a).

[64] Paul's analogy of a body is reminiscent of a similar description in Ephesians 4:16. "Supported" (NIV), "nourished" (NRSV), "having nourishment ministered" (KJV) is *epichorēgeō*, "to provide what is necessary for the well-being of another, support" (BDAG 387, 3). "Held together" (NIV, NRSV), "knit together" (KJV) is *symbibazō*, "to bring together into a unit, unite," literally, of the body, which is "held together" by sinews, ligaments, joints." (BDAG 957, 1a), figuratively, "unite, knit together." "Grows" (NIV, NRSV), "increaseth" (KJV) is *auxanō*, "to become greater, grow, increase" (BDAG 152, 2a). *Auxēsis* is "growth, increase" (BDAG 152).

[65] *Stoicheion*, "transcendent powers that are in control over events in this world, elements, elemental spirits." We discussed this word in 2:8. (BDAG 946, 2).

[66] "Submit to rules/regulations" (NIV, NRSV), "(be) subject to ordinances" (KJV) is *dogmatizō*, "to put under obligation by rules or ordinances, obligate," here in the passive (BDAG 254).

[67] "Perish" is *phthora*, with the preposition *eis*, "unto, destined to." *Phthora* refers to, "breakdown of organic matter, dissolution, deterioration, corruption," in the world of nature (BDAG 105, 1).

[68] "Appearance" (NIV, NRSV), "shew" (KJV) is *logos*, "word," here, probably has the idea of a "report, story" ("have the appearance of wisdom, pass for wisdom") or perhaps, "make a case for wisdom" (BDAG 603, 1aβ and 2f).

1. **The picky rules are not spiritual, but related to temporal matters – foods, etc. – that will pass away.** In baptism, the Colossians had died to their old way of life. Now they were being enticed to trade their new path for the old. The rules Paul writes against seem to reflect Jewish laws about ritual purity regarding unclean foods. Their world was limited by what they were not allowed to do.[69]

2. **The rules don't come from God, but from human commands and traditions.** Paul refers to them as a "self-made religion."[70]

3. **The rules don't bring about spiritual transformation.** The false teachers possess a kind of pious humility[71] and asceticism – "harsh treatment of the body."[72] Like all highly legalistic religions that are scrupulous to keep all the rules, the false teachers assume that they are somehow more spiritual. After all, they can document their faithfulness by the multitude of observances. However, none of this is of value in really changing from a body-centered life to a spiritual life. The phrase "restraining sensual indulgence" (NIV), "checking self-indulgence" (NRSV), and "the satisfying of the flesh" (KJV) translate two words *sarx*, "flesh" and *plēsmonē*, "process of securing complete satisfaction, satiety."[73]

Legalistic religions are attractive. After all, their adherents seem serious and observant. But the real question is: Do they help a person draw closer to Christ in their daily life, their character, and their actions? If not, they are empty and deceptive, for they promise something they can't deliver.

---

[69] "Handle" or "touch" is *haptō*, which carries the connotation, "to partake of something" with cultic implications, "have contact with, touch." (BDAG 126, 3). "Taste" is *geuomai*, "to partake of something by mouth, taste, partake of" (BDAG 195, 1). "Touch" or "handle" is *thinganō*, "touch" (BDAG 456).

[70] "Self-imposed worship" (NIV), "self-imposed piety" (NRSV), "will worship" (KJV) is *ethelothrēskia*, "self-made religion, do-it-yourself religion, idiosyncratic religion," perhaps, "would-be religion." (BDAG 276), from *thelō*, "desire, wish" + *thrēskeia*, "religion, worship."

[71] "False humility" (NIV), "humility" (NRSV, KJV) is *tapeinophrosynē*, "humility, modesty" (BDAG 989).

[72] "Harsh treatment" (NIV), "severe treatment" (NRSV), "neglect" (KJV) is *apheidia* (from *apheidēs*, "unsparing") from the sense "spare nothing," that is, to lavish on something, there is a transference to "sparing very little for something," as in "severe treatment of the body" (= asceticism) (BDAG 155).

[73] "Especially with food and drink, but also with other types of enjoyment, "satisfaction, gratification" (*Plēsmonē*, BDAG 830). BDAG notes: "The Greek exegetes understood this to mean for the gratification of physical needs. But *sarx*, according to verse 18, is surely to be taken in a pejorative sense, and *pros* has the force "against". The translation is probably best made along the lines of NRSV: "of no value in checking self-indulgence."

Christianity at its very core is a connection to Jesus Christ – Creator, Messiah, Son of God, Redeemer, Lover of our souls. Various spiritual practices may *aid* our devotion, but they are not the core. Jesus is!

Q4. (Colossians 2:20-23) Why are legalism and asceticism unable to restrain the sinful nature? What alternative to legalism does Paul offer in Colossians 2?
http://www.joyfulheart.com/forums/index.php?showtopic=976

In this lesson Paul has put the spotlight on Jesus Christ himself. Union with Christ by faith and baptism completes us. We don't need other observances to complete us. They are external, man-made traditions. The real substance is Christ himself. We are complete in Him. Hallelujah!

Prayer

Father, help us see Jesus more clearly than we ever have before. Help us to see him as our Completor, in whom we find completion. Thank you for your love and salvation that plucked us out of our confusion and brought us to Christ himself. In his holy name, we pray. Amen.

Key Verses

"God made you alive with Christ. He forgave us all our sins, having canceled the written code, with its regulations, that was against us and that stood opposed to us; he took it away, nailing it to the cross." (Colossians 2:13b-14, NIV)

"And having disarmed the powers and authorities, he made a public spectacle of them, triumphing over them by the cross." (Colossians 2:15, NIV)

"These are a shadow of the things that were to come; the reality, however, is found in Christ." (Colossians 2:17, NIV)

6. Guidelines for Holy Living (Colossians 3:1-17)

Much like Paul's Letter to the Ephesians, the first half of Colossians lays the theological basis, while the second half provides practical instructions for Christian living. If you see this as New Covenant Law, then you're missing the point. Paul isn't giving us regulations, but guidelines that allow the Spirit to work in us and through us.

Set Your Mind on Things Above (3:1-2)

It all begins with an attitude of heart and mind.

> "[1] Since, then, you have been raised with Christ, set your hearts on things above, where Christ is seated at the right hand of God. [2] Set your minds on things above, not on earthly things." (3:1-2)

The classic example of a loving lifestyle is caring for those who are in need. Vincent van Gogh (1853-1890), "The Good Samaritan" (1890, after Delacroix), oil on canvas, Kröller-Müller Museum, Otterlo, Netherlands.

"Since then" (NIV) or "so if" (NRSV) refers back to Paul's teaching on baptism and being raised with Christ in 2:12-13. Paul grounds his ethical instructions in the regenerative work of God's Spirit in us – "you have been raised with Christ."

Verses 1 and 2 call us to make conscious decisions about the way we think – "set your hearts/minds" (NIV, NRSV), "set your affections" (KJV). The verb is *phroneō*, "to give careful consideration to something, set one's mind on, be intent."[1] Consider these uses of the same verb in the NRSV, which is fairly consistent in translating the word:

---

[1] *Phroneō*, BDAG 106, 2a. The word *phroneō* has a wide range of meanings, "to be minded," either of reflection or of purpose. (Liddell-Scott). So it can mean (1) "think about, hold an opinion on," (2) "be intent

"[Jesus] rebuked Peter and said, 'Get behind me, Satan! For you are **setting your mind** not on divine things but on human things.'" (Mark 8:33)

"**Let the same mind be in you** that was in Christ Jesus." (Philippians 2:5)

"... Their **minds are set** on earthly things." (Philippians 3:19)

"Those who live according to the flesh **set their minds** on the things of the flesh, but those who live according to the Spirit **set their minds** on the things of the Spirit. To **set the mind** on the flesh is death, but to **set the mind** on the Spirit is life and peace. For this reason the **mind that is set on the flesh** is hostile to God; it does not submit to God's law—indeed it cannot, and those who are in the flesh cannot please God." (Romans 8:5-8)

Part of discipleship, Paul tells the Colossians, is deciding where our minds will go and where they won't. We must make this conscious decision perhaps several times a day as temptations come up.

What are we to think about? "Things above," which is symbolic of heaven and God's way. If you have frequent thought temptations, in order to retrain your mind you might decide in advance what you'll chose to think about when that lustful or hateful or proud thought flashes into your mind.

Q1. (Colossians 3:1-2) What does it mean to "set your heart/mind" on the things above? Does this mean that we're "too heavenly minded to be of any earthly good"? If not, what *does* it mean? What happens when we don't take control and direct our thinking and meditating?

http://www.joyfulheart.com/forums/index.php?showtopic=977

---

on" (as in our verses), or (3) "to develop an attitude based on careful thought, be minded/disposed" as in Philippians 2:5.

You Have Died (3:3-4)

Why should we control our thoughts and keep them focused in godly channels? Paul's answer is that we have changed. The "location" of our life is now different.

> "³ For you died, and your life is now hidden with Christ in God. ⁴ When Christ, who is your life, appears, then you also will appear with him in glory." (3:3-4)

"You died"[2] refers to our new birth in Christ, symbolized by our baptism (2:12), when we were buried with Christ and raised with Christ. This is not just figurative language. Paul is speaking of actual spiritual changes that took place in us when we repented of our sins and received Christ into our lives. This concept of death with Christ occurs several times in Paul's letters:

> "Since you **died with Christ** to the basic principles of this world, why, as though you still belonged to it, do you submit to its rules." (2:20)

> "I have been **crucified with Christ** and I no longer live, but Christ lives in me. The life I live in the body, I live by faith in the Son of God, who loved me and gave himself for me." (Galatians 2:20)

Paul develops these thoughts most thoroughly in Romans 6:1-11.[3]

Your Life Is Hid (3:3-4)

Why should you set your mind on the things of God? Because your old life is dead, and your new life is now found only in Christ. He is your present and your future!

> "³ For you died, and your life is now **hidden** with Christ in God. ⁴ When Christ, who is your life, appears, then you also will **appear** with him in glory." (3:3-4)

"Hidden/hid" is *kryptō* (from which we get our words "crypt" and "cryptography"), "to keep from being seen, hide."[4] It may not appear to others that your life is in Christ. It is hidden. But it is still true! We are in a different realm – with Christ, in God. The sooner we grasp this and begin to act accordingly, the easier the Christian life will become.

---

[2] "Died/are dead" is *apothnēskō*, "to cease to have vital functions, whether at an earthly or transcendent level, die." (BDAG 113, 1bβ). The word is in the Aorist tense, past tense at a particular point in time.

[3] I've spent considerable time seeking to explain this in my book *Christ Powered Life: Romans 5-8* (JesusWalk Publications, 2008).

[4] *Kryptō*, BDAG 573, 1d.

This hiddenness will finally be revealed when Christ returns in Glory. Hidden is just the opposite of "appear" or "revealed"[5] in verse 4. The following verses also speak of the final revealing of our true state:

> "But our citizenship is in heaven. And we eagerly await a Savior from there, the Lord Jesus Christ." (Philippians 3:20)

> "Dear friends, now we are children of God, and what we will be has not yet been made known. But we know that when he appears, we shall be like him, for we shall see him as he is." (1 John 3:2)

Put to Death Your Old Practices (3:5-8)

Because our true identity is now in Christ and not in our old life, it makes sense that we begin to roll this truth into our whole lives. When a large chain of stores comes under new ownership, it may take a few months or even years to change over the signage and policies and culture to that of the new corporation, but eventually, it must take place for the new store to claim its rightful brand.

> "⁵ **Put to death**, therefore, whatever belongs to your earthly nature: sexual immorality, impurity, lust, evil desires and greed, which is idolatry. ⁶ Because of these, the wrath of God is coming. ⁷ You used to walk in these ways, in the life you once lived. ⁸ But now you must **rid yourselves** of all such things as these: anger, rage, malice, slander, and filthy language from your lips." (3:5-8)

Paul uses two verbs to describe the brand-changing process: "put to death" and "rid yourselves."

- **"Put to death"** (NIV, NRSV), "mortify" (KJV) in verse 5 is *nekroō*, from *nekros*, "dead" (which shows up in several English words that begin with "necro-"). The verb means literally, "to make something dead."[6] Similar ideas are found in Romans 8:13; Galatians 5:24; Titus 2:12; and 2 Corinthians 7:1.

- **"Rid yourselves of"** (NIV), "get rid of" (NRSV), "put off" (KJV) in verse 8 is *apotithēmi*, "take off," literally to take off one's clothes. Then figuratively, to "lay

---

[5] "Appear/s" (NIV, KJV), "revealed" (NRSV), which appears twice in verse 4, is *phaneroō*, "to cause to become visible, reveal, expose publicly" (BDAG 104, 1aβ).

[6] *Nekroō* means, "to deaden or cause to cease completely, put to death." A figurative extension of the primary meaning is, "to put an end to the life of something, to cause to be dead" (BDAG 668).

aside, rid oneself."[7] Similar language is used in Colossians 3:8; Ephesians 4:22, 25; Hebrews 12:1; James 1:21; and 1 Peter 2:1.

The words are essentially used synonymously; Paul varies the verbs for the sake of variety. These words present a very active idea – something we must initiate and carry out, aided, of course, by the Holy Spirit.

Sinful Behaviors (3:5-8)

We shouldn't feel insulted if Paul's instructions about sin seem pretty basic. Paul was writing to a primarily Gentile church in a culture that didn't have much concept of sin at all. Let's consider these sins one at a time:

Put to Death Sexual Sins (3:5-6)

"Sexual immorality" (NIV), **"fornication"** (NRSV, KJV) is *porneia*, from which we get our word "pornography". It means, "unlawful sexual intercourse, prostitution, unchastity, fornication."[8] A *pornē* was a prostitute or harlot. The KJV tends to translate *porneia* as "fornication," but this is too narrow. "Fornication" is defined in English as "consensual sexual intercourse between two persons not married to each other."[9] *Porneia*, on the other hand, includes not only fornication, but adultery, homosexuality, and any other kind of imaginable sexual perversion.

I once had a couple in my church who became fond of each other and then became engaged to be married. Both of them loved the Lord. Both were children of the '60s. The man had grown up in the California surfer culture and sex between two people who loved one another seemed right to him. She wasn't so sure. I patiently explained what the scripture taught from Old Testament to New, but he couldn't see it. His culture had blinded him. However, he said, "Pastor, though I don't see anything in the Bible against sex before marriage, I'll abstain because you say so. His bride looked relieved. And eventually they were married, and enjoy, I am sure, the joys of marriage together.

Paul is even more specific in 1 Thessalonians as he instructs a pagan culture in ways of holiness:

> "It is God's will that you should be sanctified: that you should avoid sexual immorality; that each of you should learn to control his own body in a way that is holy

---

[7] *Apotithēmi*, BDAG 123, 1b.

[8] *Porneia*, BDAG 854, 1. Also Friedrich Hauck and Siegfried Schulz, *pornē, ktl.*, TDNT 6:579-595.

[9] *Merriam-Webster's 11th Collegiate Dictionary*.

and honorable, not in passionate lust like the heathen, who do not know God; and that in this matter no one should wrong his brother or take advantage of him. The Lord will punish men for all such sins, as we have already told you and warned you. For God did not call us to be impure, but to live a holy life. Therefore, he who rejects this instruction does not reject man but God, who gives you his Holy Spirit." (1 Thessalonians 4:3-8)

This runs directly against our culture, which says that sex between consenting adults is okay. We don't have to condemn and put down all those around us who live loosely, but we need to hold high standards for ourselves, and see that our churches hold high standards for members.

"Impurity" (NIV, NRSV), **"uncleanness"** (KJV) is *akatharsia*, literally, "any substance that is filthy or dirty, refuse," figuratively, "a state of moral corruption, immorality, vileness," especially used of sexual sins.[10]

"Lust" (NIV), "passion" (NRSV), "inordinate affection" (KJV) is *pathos*, "experience of strong desire, passion."[11] The word doesn't have to refer to sexual sin, but does here and in its two other New Testament occurrences (Romans 1:26 and 1 Thessalonians 4:5).

"Evil desires" (NIV, NRSV), "evil concupiscence" (KJV) is *epithymia*. The word can be used for positive desire, but here it is, "a desire for something forbidden or simply inordinate, craving, lust."[12] In the context, these words probably have a sexual connotation.

"Greed" (NIV, NRSV), "covetousness" (KJV) is *pleonexia*, "the inappropriate desire for more."[13] In some contexts, this refers to the desire for more money, but in this context it could also refer to the insatiable desire for sexual pleasure, or greed for one more sexual conquest. Whenever we put sex (or wealth or anything else) on the pedestal of our greatest goal, it becomes a false god to us, and makes us guilty of idolatry.

In our world it is common to try to rationalize sexual sins as merely normal human desires. It is quite true that the desire for sex is a strong, innate drive. And surely God created this drive, for it fuels his command to "be fruitful and multiply" (Genesis 1:28).

But to suppose that God is neutral about how we exercise our sexuality runs directly in the face of Scripture. He has given us an arena in which we can exercise our sexuality

[10] *Akatharsia*, BDAG 34, 2.
[11] *Pathos*, BDAG 748, 2.
[12] *Epithymia*, BDAG 372, 2.
[13] Moo, *Colossians*, p. 257. The state of desiring to have more than one's due, greediness, insatiableness, avarice, covetousness" (*Pleonexia*, BDAG 824).

freely – the bonds of marriage. Outside of the bounds of marriage, sex can become destructive – to children and families, for example. Sexual sins outside of marriage, both of the body and of the mind, can become compulsive and dangerous. So we are to put to death in us the permission to exercise our sexuality outside of the bounds of marriage.

Then, lest we rationalize our behaviors in order to permit ourselves these things, Paul reminds us:

> "⁶ Because of these, the wrath of God is coming. ⁷ You used to walk in these ways, in the life you once lived." (2:6-7)

These sins belong to your former life, not your new life.

Q2. (Colossians 3:5) Why is sexual lust so difficult for people, especially males? Though we cannot deny that we are sexual beings, how can we keep sexual desire from controlling us and causing us to sin?
http://www.joyfulheart.com/forums/index.php?showtopic=978

Put Off the Sins of Anger and the Tongue (3:8)

The next list of sins relates to unrestrained anger and the damage it causes through our tongues.

> "But now you must rid yourselves of all such things as these: anger, rage, malice, slander, and filthy language from your lips." (2:8)

Let's consider the words

"Anger" in verse 8 is *orgē*, the "state of relatively strong displeasure, with focus on the emotional aspect, anger."[14] Anger is a God-given emotion that moves us to action when we are treated unjustly. Without it we might be passive to great evil. There is "righteous anger," a correct response to injustice – though often our anger is based more on selfish reactions that put us at a disadvantage, rather than based on a reaction to sin.

---

[14] *Orgē*, BDAG 720, 1.

It is also possible to experience the emotion of anger without sin. Paul writes to the Ephesian church (quoting Psalm 4:4):

> "'In your anger do not sin': Do not let the sun go down while you are still angry, and do not give the devil a foothold." (Ephesians 4:26-27)

So anger, in and of itself, is not sin. But anger has a way of loosening our inhibitions, making it much more likely that we will do something or say something that we will regret later. Paul warns us of unrestrained anger.

Anger can also dwell in us for long periods of time if we allow it to. Victims of sexual abuse or returning soldiers with post-traumatic stress disorder (PTSD), for example, can have their lives destroyed by anger. Sometimes we need help in how to let go of our anger so it doesn't poison our relationships and ruin our lives.

"Rage" (NIV), **"wrath"** (NRSV, KJV) in verse 8 is *thymos*, "a state of intense displeasure, anger, wrath, rage, indignation."[15] Vincent states the shade of difference between *orgē* and *thymos* in this way: "*Orgē* denotes a deeper and more permanent sentiment; a settled habit of mind; while *thymos* is a more turbulent, but temporary agitation."[16] Perhaps rage or wrath describe us when our anger flares up and becomes loud and perhaps violent. "Rid yourselves" of this, Paul says. The Holy Spirit can help you tame your anger, but you must humbly allow him to work.

"Malice" in verse 8 is *kakia*, "wickedness," here, "a mean-spirited or vicious attitude or disposition, malice, ill-will, malignity."[17] You've seen this terrible motivation in others' behavior. Has it afflicted you – especially in relation to certain people in your life?

"Slander" (NIV, NRSV), **"blasphemy"** (KJV) is *blasphēmia*, "speech that denigrates or defames, reviling, denigration, disrespect, slander."[18] We get our word "blaspheme" from this Greek word. This could refer to using God's or Jesus' name in a curse. But more likely here it means the kind of terrible things we say about people when we are angry at them. In English we have three words which describe such behavior:

- **Slander** – "the utterance of false charges or misrepresentations which defame and damage another's reputation."

---

[15] *Thymos*, BDAG 461, 2.
[16] Vincent, *Word Studies*, at John 3:36.
[17] *Kakia*, BDAG 500, 2.
[18] *Blasphēmia*, BDAG 178, a.

- **Libel** – "a written or oral defamatory statement or representation that conveys an unjustly unfavorable impression."

- **Gossip** – "a rumor or report of an intimate nature."[19]

I've caught myself relaying information that puts someone in an unfavorable light, when I should have kept my mouth shut. But anger and unforgiveness often feed talk that defames and hurts. We are to rid ourselves of this destructive habit!

"Filthy language" (NIV), "abusive language" (NRSV), "filthy communication" (KJV) is *aischrologia*, "speech of a kind that is generally considered in poor taste, obscene speech, dirty talk," perhaps "scurrilous talk," especially since *blasphēmia* immediately precedes.[20] This compound word is derived from *aischros*, "base, dishonorable, shameful" + *logos*, "speech." This word covers all sorts of speech that is punctuated by sexual terms and bathroom language. This is the way the world talks, not we followers of Jesus Christ the Lord.

We must rid ourselves of this kind of language. When we slip into our old vocabulary, we stop, ask forgiveness of God and any who may have heard us, and then substitute a more appropriate expression. After a dozen or several dozen repetitions of this process, our vocabulary gets much cleaner. Oh, we may slip occasionally, but it will no longer be our normal manner of expression.

We can't isolate ourselves from people who talk this way, as if we are too holy to hear such words. Nor should we be constantly putting them down for their crude speech, as if we are the language police for our sector of the world – in your home maybe, but not in the marketplace where you don't have the authority to set the rules. We live in this world, but are not of it. What's more, the people who talk this way need our Savior desperately. But our vocabulary needs to be cleansed so that it reflects well on our Master. They will notice.

---

[19] *Merriam-Webster 11th Collegiate Dictionary* (Merriam-Webster, 1993).
[20] *Aischrologia*, BDAG 29.

Q3. (Colossians 3:8) Why are sins of the tongue so easy to slip into? In what ways do they damage us and others? How can we break free of sins of the tongue? http://www.joyfulheart.com/forums/index.php?showtopic=979

Don't Lie (3:9)

Next, Paul touches a problem that afflicts us Christians far too often. Lying.

"Do not lie to each other, since you have taken off your old self with its practices." (3:9)

"Lie" is *pseudomai*, "to tell a falsehood, lie."[21] What makes lying wrong? Satan is known as "the father of lies" (John 8:44). Our God, on the other hand, is a God of truth. Our faith in God is based on us trusting him completely. Lying is utterly contrary to God's nature. And we have "taken off" our old self with its evil practices and are being renewed in God's image.

We know that trust builds community, builds marriages, builds relationships. Lying, by its very nature, undermines and explodes marriages and relationships. It destroys communities. Yes, there may be special circumstances in times of war -- or admiring a woman's ugly dress. But Paul is not speaking of the exceptions, but of the practice of truthful speech in contrast to angry, slanderous, abusive speech.

The New Self, Being Renewed (3:9-10)

Let's explore this idea of renewal further:

"9 Do not lie to each other, since you have **taken off** your old self with its practices 10 and have put on the new self, which is **being renewed** in knowledge in the image of its Creator." (3:9-10)

---

[21] *Pseudomai*, BDAG 1097, 1. It is derived from *pseudos*, "falsehood," from which we get our prefix "pseudo-".

Paul's analogy in verses 9 and 10 is taking off[22] and putting on[23] clothing. In Christ we have changed clothes. But the change is not just external, but internal, in our spirit and in our character. No, it is not instantaneous. We are "being renewed," that is, literally, "made new again."[24] Praise God! This is the process of sanctification. We see several other uses of the word in Paul's letters:

> "Though outwardly we are wasting away, yet inwardly we are **being renewed** day by day." (2 Corinthians 4:16b)

> "He saved us through the washing of rebirth and **renewal** by the Holy Spirit." (Titus 3:5b)

> "Be transformed by the **renewing** of your mind." (Romans 12:2b)

We are obviously to cooperate in the process of renewal, rather than thwart it by our obstinate rebelliousness. But ultimately it is God's work in us, the fruit of the Holy Spirit of God. The renewal involves our mind, as we take hold of and internalize God's truths (knowledge[25]). But the goal is far beyond ourselves; it is to restore God's image[26] in us that has been marred and fallen through sin. God wants to renew us all the way back to his original creation:

> "So God created man in his own image,
> in the image of God he created him;
> male and female he created them." (Genesis 1:27)

In a number of passages in the Bible, we see our final destiny to be found as restored to our original perfect state in the Garden of God (Luke 23:43 and 2 Corinthians 12:4, where "Paradise" means "garden"; Revelation 2:7; 22:2, 14, 19).

---

[22] "Taken off" (NIV), "stripped off" (NRSV), "put off" (KJV) is *apekdyomai*, which we saw in 2:15 ("disarming" the principalities and powers). The basic meaning is "to take off, strip off," of clothes. Here it is used figuratively (BDAG 100, 1).

[23] "Put on" (NIV, KJV), "clothed yourselves with" (NRSV) is *endyō* (from which we get our English word, "endue"). It means, "to put clothing or apparel on someone, *endyō*, clothe someone." It is used figuratively here an at 3:12 (BDAG 333, 2b). We see a similar uses in Ephesians 4:24; Romans 13:14; and Galatians 3:27. In Luke 24:49 it is used of the baptism of the Holy Spirit: "clothed" (NIV, NRSV) or "endued" (KJV) with power from on high.

[24] "Renewed" is *anakainoō*, from *ana-*, "again" + *kainoō*, "make new" (BDAG 64). The noun is *anakainōsis*, "renewal."

[25] "Knowledge" is *epignōsis*, "knowledge, recognition" (BDAG 369).

[26] "Image" is *eikōn* (which we saw in 1:15, from which we get our word "icon"), "that which represents something else in terms of basic form and features, form, appearance" (BDAG 282, 2).

What are you doing that enables the process of renewal in your heart? What are you doing that hinders that process of renewal?

One in Christ (3:11)

We no longer lie to each other, says Paul, because we are one in Christ. People lie to protect themselves from those who are different from them, who might threaten them. But you are one, says Paul:

> "Here there is no Greek or Jew, circumcised or uncircumcised, barbarian, Scythian, slave or free, but Christ is all, and is in all." (3:11)

Greeks worshipped many gods, Jews worshipped one God. But now they are one in Christ. Jews took great pride in circumcision as a symbol of their distinctiveness as people of the Covenant. It separated them from all others. But now we are one in Christ.

"Barbarian" referred to a non-Greek, a foreigner.[27] A Scythian lived in the region of the Black Sea and was viewed as the epitome of unrefinement or savagery.[28] But Christ unites both! Slave and free were common divisions in the world of Paul's day. In fact, many Christians were slaves. But in Christ we are one! There are no divisions, nor may we allow divisions to arise.[29]

Cloth Yourselves with Virtue (3:12)

No longer divided by race, religion, geographical origin, social status, or gender, the church is special:

> "Therefore, as God's chosen people, holy and dearly loved, clothe yourselves with compassion, kindness, humility, gentleness and patience." (3:12)

See how we are described:

- **Chosen**, "the elect of God" (KJV), is *eklektos*, "pertaining to being selected, chosen."[30]

---

[27] *Barbaros*, "a non-Hellene, foreigner." Our similar word, "barbarian" is frequently used in a negative sense, which the Greek word doesn't necessarily imply (BDAG 166, 2b). This word is *not* related etymologically to "barber, beard."

[28] *Skythēs*, BDAG 932.

[29] In Galatians, Paul adds male and female to such a list: "[28] There is neither Jew nor Greek, slave nor free, male nor female, for you are all one in Christ Jesus." (Galatians 3:28)

[30] *Eklektos*, BDAG 306, 1.

- **Holy**, *hagios*, means "dedicated to God, holy, sacred, that is, reserved for God and God's service."[31]

- **Beloved**, *agapaō*, "loved." Think of the immense status there is in being greatly loved and cherished by the Creator of the Universe and the Savior of Mankind!

Because we are God's people, we are to clothe ourselves with the character of Christ. We are to take off the old clothes and to put on the new clothes, the Christian virtues that bring honor to our Savior.

"Compassion" (NIV, NRSV), "bowels of mercies" (KJV) is actually two words in Greek: *splanchnon*, "inward parts, entrails," thought of in the ancient world as the seat of the emotions,"[32] and *oiktirmos*, "display of concern over another's misfortune, pity, mercy, compassion." The two words together might be translated "heartfelt compassion."[33] We are to be a people marked by a sincere and ready compassion.

"Kindness" is *chrēstotēs*, "the quality of being helpful or beneficial, goodness, kindness, generosity."[34] This is one of the fruits of the Spirit (Galatians 5:22).

"Humility" (NIV, NRSV), "humbleness of mind" (KJV) is *tapeinophrosynē*, "humility, modesty,"[35] "the having a humble opinion of oneself; a deep sense of one's (moral) littleness; modesty, humility, lowliness of mind."[36] We aren't to feign humility of the surface, self-deprecating Uriah Heep sort. Rather, we are to live in the knowledge that what we have received is a gift, not a reward for our greatness. Thankfulness is present in a humble person.

"Gentleness" (NIV), **"meekness"** (NRSV, KJV) is a related idea. The Greek word is *prautēs*, "the quality of not being overly impressed by a sense of one's self-importance, gentleness, humility, courtesy, considerateness, meekness" in the older favorable sense.[37] This is also a fruit of the Spirit (Galatians 5:23). This doesn't mean a poor self-image. Rather it is the characteristic of a person who doesn't feel the need to impress others and force oneself on others.

---

[31] *Hagios*, BDAG 10, 1aβaleph.
[32] *Splanchnon*, BDAG 938, 2.
[33] *Oiktirmos*, BDAG 700.
[34] *Chrēstotēs*, BDAG 1090, 2a.
[35] *Tapeinophrosynē*, BDAG 989.
[36] *Tapeinophrosynē*, Thayer. from *tapeinos*, "low" + *phrēn*, "the mind."
[37] *Prautēs*, BDAG 861.

"**Patience**" (NIV, NRSV), "longsuffering" (KJV) is *makrothymia*, from *makros*, "long" + *thumos*, "passion." It means, the "state of being able to bear up under provocation, forbearance, patience toward others."[38] This is also a fruit of the Spirit (Galatians 5:22).

What a beautiful set of characteristics that adorn a person with the beauty of Christ!

Forgive Each Other (3:13)

Now Paul mentions two character qualities that are necessary for a healthy Christian community – whether it be a church or a family: forbearance and forgiveness.

"Bear with each other and forgive whatever grievances[39] you may have against one another. Forgive as the Lord forgave you." (3:13)

"**Bear with**" (NIV, NIV), "forbearing" (KJV) is *anechō*, "to regard with tolerance, endure, bear with, put up with."[40] We see a similar exhortation in Ephesians:

"Be completely humble and gentle; be patient, bearing with one another in love." (Ephesians 4:2)

Forbearance doesn't require forgiveness. It requires tolerance, patience, and love. We're all different. We have quirks and idiosyncrasies that can drive each other crazy. And so often we're blind to them ourselves. Forbearance is the willingness to put up with each others' differences.

"**Forgive/forgiving,**" is used twice in this verse. It is the ability to forgive not just differences, but sins against us. The verb is *charizomai*, which we saw in 2:13, "to show oneself gracious by forgiving wrongdoing, forgive, pardon."[41] So long as we are constantly clamoring to be "right," we will destroy community. In our quest to be vindicated, we can easily destroy. Often, to preserve the community, the marriage, the family, we must forgive sins and refuse to hold them against the person any longer. God will bring justice in the end. It's not our job.

Love (3:14)

"And over all these virtues put on love, which binds them all together in perfect unity." (3:14)

---

[38] *Makrothymia*, BDAG 612, 2a.
[39] "Grievances" (NIV) "complaint" (NRSV), "quarrel" (KJV) is *momphē*, "blame, (cause for) complaint" (BDAG 657).
[40] *Anechō*, BDAG 78, 1a.
[41] *Charizomai*, BDAG 1078, 3.

Verse 14 begins "upon all these things." Paul seems to be continuing his metaphor of putting on garments from verse 12 – "clothe yourselves with...." So love[42] would be the outer cloak or overcoat put on "over" (*epi*) all the others that unifies them. The phrase "binds together in perfect unity/harmony" (NIV, NRSV), or "bond of perfectness" (KJV) is two words, *syndesmos* ("bond")[43] and *teleiotēs* ("perfection").[44]

Q4. (Colossians 3:12-14) Why are Christian virtues so important to Christ? Why are they so important to the church? Why are they so important to non-Christians? Why are they so important in our homes?
http://www.joyfulheart.com/forums/index.php?showtopic=980

Peace and Thankfulness (3:15)

The result of the Christian virtues capped by love is peace.

"Let the peace of Christ rule in your hearts, since as members of one body you were called to peace. And be thankful." (3:15)

"Peace" is used twice in the verse, as if to emphasize it. "Rule" is *brabeuō*, not the usual word for "rule." Originally it referred to the referee or umpire who would "award prizes in contests." Here it means by extension, "be in control of someone's activity by making a decision, be judge, decide, control, rule."[45] Peace is to "call the shots." It is the standard of keeping unity within the body. We are different members of the body, but we are members of the same body, so we should not war with ourselves. God calls us to peace. In Ephesians, Paul put it another way:

---

[42] "Love" (NIV, NRSV), "charity" (KJV) is *agapē*, "the quality of warm regard for and interest in another, esteem, affection, regard, love" (BDAG 6, 1aα).

[43] "Binds together in unity/harmony" (NIV, NRSV), "bond" (KJV) is *syndesmos*, "that which holds something together, fastener," here, "that which brings various entities into a unified relationship, uniting bond" (BDAG 966).

[44] "Perfect" (NIV), "perfectness" (KJV), is *teleiotēs*, "perfection, completeness" (BDAG 996) from *teleios*, "attaining an end or purpose, complete."

[45] *Brabeuō*, BDAG 183.

"Make every effort to keep the unity of the Spirit through the bond of peace."
(Ephesians 4:3)

The final virtue he mentions – almost as an afterthought -- is thankfulness: "And be thankful." "Thankful" is *eucharistos*, an adjective "pertaining to being grateful, thankful."[46] We get our word "Eucharist" from this word, because the word was used in giving thanks or blessing God for the bread and cup in the Lord's Supper (Mark 14:22-23; Luke 22:17, 19; 1 Corinthians 11:24).

Teaching, Exhorting, and Singing (3:16)

How are we to live? Not in legalism or in the flesh. Rather the Christian believers are to set their minds on the things of God, to live out and embody the Christian virtues, with peace in their community. Paul has given two exhortations for the community:

1. "Let the peace of God rule ..." (3:15) and

2. "Let the word of Christ dwell in you...." (3:16)

   "Let the word of Christ dwell in you richly as you teach and admonish one another
   with all wisdom, and as you sing psalms, hymns and spiritual songs with gratitude
   in your hearts to God." (3:16)

"Dwell in" is *enoikeō*, "live, dwell (in)."[47] "Richly" is *plousiōs*, "richly, abundantly,"[48] from *ploutos*, "wealth, abundance." Christ's words are to fill our mouths and be the center of our community.

"Teach and admonish" is a pair of words we saw earlier:

   "We proclaim him, admonishing and teaching everyone with all wisdom, so that we
   may present everyone perfect in Christ." (1:28)

"Teach" refers to the positive expression, "admonish" to the negative expression. "Admonish," *noutheteō*, means "to counsel about avoidance or cessation of an improper course of conduct, admonish, warn, instruct."[49] Positive Thinking, championed by Norman Vincent Peale (1898-1993) and later by Robert Schuller (1926-), has down-graded the idea of warning and admonishing from the pulpit. This is probably in reaction to the harsh haranguing that sometimes characterized preachers of another era.

---

[46] *Eucharistos*, BDAG 416.
[47] *Enoikeō*, BDAG 338, from *en-*, "in" + *oikeō*, "reside, inhabit."
[48] *Plousiōs*, BDAG 831.
[49] *Noutheteō*, BDAG 679.

But warning and admonishing – as well as exhorting or urging or encouraging – were certainly the practice of the early church in forming disciples. This was not only Paul's practice of training disciples (1:28). He also encourages it as part of their regular meetings together in conjunction with their singing.

Songs, Hymns, and Spiritual Songs (3:16b)

> "... As you sing psalms, hymns and spiritual songs with gratitude in your hearts to God." (3:16)

This trio of terms for songs is also found in Ephesians 5:19:

> "Speak to one another with psalms, hymns and spiritual songs. Sing and make music in your heart to the Lord, always giving thanks to God the Father for everything, in the name of our Lord Jesus Christ." (Ephesians 5:19-20)

1. **Psalms** were singing the Psalter, the book of Psalms, which was written to be sung, and was sung by the Jews in Paul's day. Though these also could have been Christian odes patterned on the Psalter.

2. **Hymns** "probably had a religious and cultic significance ... as a technical term for festive psalms of praise, and for liturgical calls and recitations."[50] Group members were encouraged to each bring a hymn or some other contribution from the Spirit when the believers gathered, in order to build up one another (1 Corinthians 14:16). These may have been longer compositions.

3. **Spiritual songs** may have been more spontaneous, perhaps like Paul's "singing in the Spirit" (1 Corinthians 14:15), though the lines between psalms, hymns, and spiritual songs are not firmly drawn. Martin says, "The terms are probably used loosely to cover the various forms of musical composition."[51]

Do Everything in the Name of Jesus (3:17)

Paul sums it all up with a final statement, one that has served as a guiding verse for me in the earlier years of my ministry:

---

[50] Karl-Heinz Bartels, "Song, Hymn, Psalm," NIDNTT 3:668-670. *Hymnos* (from which we get our word "hymn") is "a song with religious content, hymn/song of praise" especially in honor of a deity (BDAG 1027).

[51] Ralph P. Martin, *Worship in the Early Church* (revised edition, Eerdmans, 1974), pp. 39-52, with this quote on p. 47.

"And whatever you do, whether in word or deed, do it all in the name of the Lord Jesus, giving thanks to God the Father through him." (3:17)

In our culture, "name" refers primarily to what a person is called. But in Hebrew thought that underlies Paul's usage, "name" can imply "something real, a piece of the very nature of the personality whom it designates, expressing the person's qualities and powers."[52] For an Old Testament prophet to speak "in the name of the Lord" implies that he speaks on a commission from Yahweh himself. In the New Testament, words and actions "in the name of the Lord" infer that the person is acting or speaking "in the sphere of power of" or "in the presence of."[53]

So when Paul says "do it all in the name of the Lord Jesus," he is saying that we should speak and act in full consciousness of the Lord Jesus Christ. If what we are planning to do or say can't stand the test of Jesus' presence and approval without our being ashamed, then it isn't appropriate. Like Jesus' Golden Rule, this verse helps us evaluate our words and actions to see if they stand the test.

The second part of this verse asks us in all our words and deeds to act in a way that we are "giving thanks to God the Father through him." Does this deed represent thanks to God? Is this word spoken in thankfulness? If so, let it be done. If so, let it be spoken.

Is this a new Christian Law? No, Paul is presenting guidelines for living as a Christian. Paul lays out the principles:

1. Set your heart on things above (3:2).

2. Live like those who have died to the old life and look forward to the new one to be revealed (3:3-4).

3. Put to death sexual sins and sins of the tongue, which aren't appropriate to your new state (3:5-10).

4. Rather clothe yourselves with Christian virtues, especially love, and live at peace with one another (3:12-15).

5. Let your conversation and worship be full of Christ's words (3:16).

6. And let your actions and words be said and done under the view of and with the pleasure of the Lord Jesus (3:17).

---

[52] *Onoma*, BDAG, 312, 1dγ,Gimmel.
[53] Hans Bietenhardt, *onoma, ktl.*, TDNT 5:242-283, especially pp. 260, 271.

Prayer

Father, thank you for the new life we have in Christ. Thank you that we can live in the light, with peace and love and harmony. Thank you for the joy we have in this new life, and the integrity to which you call us in Christ Jesus. In his mighty name, we pray. Amen.

Key Verses

"Set your minds on things above, not on earthly things. For you died, and your life is now hidden with Christ in God." (Colossians 3:2-3, NIV)

"Bear with each other and forgive whatever grievances you may have against one another. Forgive as the Lord forgave you." (Colossians 3:13, NIV)

"And whatever you do, whether in word or deed, do it all in the name of the Lord Jesus, giving thanks to God the Father through him." (Colossians 3:17, NIV)

7. Christian Households (Colossians 3:18-4:1)

The next section isn't designed to be the last word on husband and wife roles, as some would make it out to be. These nine verses are not to be considered a comprehensive guide to household relationships. However, Paul seems to hit the hot buttons that often need help. And when God hits those buttons in *us*, we sometimes get hot too!

We see this type of brief counsel to people in various roles several times in Scripture. In

William Holman Hunt (English Pre-Raphaelite painter, 1827-1910), "A Converted British Family Sheltering a Christian Missionary from the Persecution of the Druids" (1850), oil on canvas, Ashmolean Museum, Oxford.

commentaries, this table of household roles and duties is sometimes referred to as an *Haustafel*, literally "house table," a term first used by Martin Luther. The New Testament contains three of these:

	Ephesians	Colossians	1 Peter
Wives	5:22-24	3:18	3:1-6
Husbands	5:25-33	3:19	3:7
Children	6:1-4	3:20	-
Fathers	6:4	3:21	-
Slaves	6:5-8	3:22-25	2:18-25
Masters	6:9	4:1	-

Colossians is the most abbreviated of these lists, with the most instruction given to the common situation in the New Testament world of how Christian slaves should behave.

Wives, Submit to Your Husbands (3:18)

Let's look at Paul's first brief instruction:

"Wives, submit to your husbands, as is fitting in the Lord." (3:18)

One of the areas that both Paul and Peter need to remind Christian wives about is to submit to their husbands. This is a complex topic in a Western twenty-first century context. We'll look at the principles here.

"Submit yourselves" (NIV, KJV), "be subject" (NRSV) is *hypotassō*, "to cause to be in a submissive relationship, to subject, to subordinate," here in the middle voice, "subject oneself, be subjected or subordinated, obey."[1] It is a compound word derived from *hypo*, "under" + *tassō*, "put, place." *Hypotassō*, "subordinate yourselves," has a subtle difference from "obey" (*hypakouō*) that we see with regard to children in verse 20. Here, wives are instructed to voluntarily subordinate themselves rather than to be subject to a parent's command. Voluntary submission is an honorable position that shows respect. It does not required a servile attitude, nor does it invite male domination. It does not lessen one's personhood to submit oneself – we do it in all sorts of relationships in our world. For a much fuller development of this topic see my exposition of Ephesians 5:21-33, where Paul considers the theological underpinnings of the husband-wife relationship.[2]

Notice in verse 8 three important modifiers:

- **"Husbands."** The Greek word is the plural of *anēr*, "adult male, man, husband."[3] "Wives" is the plural of *gynē*, "adult female, woman, wife."[4] Here, however, the context and the presence of definite articles in verses 19 and 20 require husband and wife (your man / your woman). Paul does not teach that all women must submit to any man or all men, but that a wife should submit to her own husband. Women are not second-class Christians.

---

[1] *Hypotassō*, BDAG 1042, 1bβ.
[2] Ralph F. Wilson, *Disciple Lessons from Ephesians* (JesusWalk, 2007), chapter 13.
[3] *Anēr*, BDAG 79, 1a.
[4] *Gynē*, BDAG 209, 2.

- **"Fitting/fit"** is *anēkō*, "it is proper, fitting."[5] Appropriate submission to one's husband is proper. However, there are types of submission which are not proper, godly, or healthy. Wives are not required to submit in such ways.
- **"In the Lord."** The submission is part of a woman's service to God and is to be carried out in that context. This is not male domination of a wife, but a voluntary submission "as is fitting in the Lord."

Husbands, Love Your Wives (3:19)

Now Paul turns to men as husbands – he speaks to them as fathers in verse 21. Sometimes men only want to read verse 18 about their wife's responsibility, but neglect their own.

"Husbands, love your wives and do not be harsh with them." (3:19)

"Love" is *agapaō*, "to have a warm regard for and interest in another, cherish, have affection for, love."[6] The problem we often face in families is a husband who demands submission from his wife, but doesn't really love her or have her interests at heart. This doesn't work well. The husband must have an unselfish love for his wife for a Christian marriage to thrive. Grow up, men!

"Be harsh" (NIV), "treat harshly" (NRSV), "be bitter" (KJV) is *pikrainō*, from which we get our word "picric acid," that is, bitter acid. It means, "to cause bitter feelings, embitter, make bitter," in an affective sense. Passive "become bitter" or "embittered."[7] Sometimes when a wife doesn't behave the way her husband wants, he gets sharp and bitter in the way he treats her. Don't do it, says Paul.

Husbands, we are commanded in both a positive and a negative way. Positive: *Do* love your wife unselfishly. Negative: *Do not* speak or act with bitterness toward her.

---

[5] *Anēkō*, BDAG 79, 2.
[6] *Agapaō*, BDAG 5, 1aα.
[7] *Pikrainō* BDAG 812, 2.

Q1. (Colossians 3:18-19) Why do you think Paul chose these directions to give to wives and husbands – considering all the things he could have said? Why is true submission difficult for wives? Why is unselfish love difficult for husbands? What prompts harshness in a husband? Is the cause inner or outer?
http:/www.joyfulheart.com/forums/index.php?showtopic=981

Children, Obey Your Parents (3:20)

Now Paul speaks to children:

"Children, obey your parents in everything, for this pleases the Lord." (3:20)

The children[8] spoken to here are minor children, not adult children. We are to honor our parents always (Exodus 20:12), but we are to obey them "in all things" when we are in their household. At marriage, "a man will leave his father and mother and be united to his wife, and the two will become one flesh" (Matthew 19:5, quoting Genesis 2:24).

"Obey" here (and with regard to slaves in verse 22) is *hypakouō*, "to follow instructions, obey, follow, be subject to,"[9] from *hypo-*, "under" + *akouō*, "hear." Children are literally under their parents' commands. They are to hear and obey.

This is not just a natural duty, says Paul. Children are to obey their parents because it "pleases[10] the Lord."

Fathers, Don't Provoke Your Children (3:21)

Paul looks at both sides of each of these relationships – wife/husband, child/parent/father, slave/master. Here his instruction to fathers is:

"Fathers, do not embitter your children, or they will become discouraged." (3:21)

"Embitter" (NIV), "provoke" (NRSV, KJV), is *erethizō*, "to cause someone to react in a way that suggests acceptance of a challenge, arouse, provoke," mostly in bad sense,

---

[8] *Teknon*, "an offspring of human parents, child" (BDAG 994, 1a).

[9] *Hypakouō*, BDAG 1028, 1.

[10] "Pleases" (NIV), "acceptable duty" (NRSV), "well pleasing" (KJV) is *euarestos*, "pleasing, acceptable" (BDAG 403).

"irritate, embitter."[11] I'm sure that mothers can arouse anger in their children, too – and to the degree that this is true, Paul's injunction applies to them, as well. However, it seems like it is more often fathers (at least in our culture) that tend to be more distant from their children and sometimes impose harsh, impractical laws upon them.

Be careful, says Paul. The effect can be that they "become/be discouraged" (NIV, KJV) or "lose heart" (NRSV). The verb is *athymeō*, "to become disheartened to the extent of losing motivation, be discouraged, lose heart, become dispirited."[12] It is one thing to punish misbehavior. But we must not seek to break the spirits of our children, for then hopelessness can set in, causing far more long-lasting effects than simple misbehavior. Be careful, Paul warns.

Q2. (Colossians 3:20-21) In what way does obedience prepare a child for everyday life in the future? For spiritual life in the future? What can fathers do to keep from discouraging their children?

http://www.joyfulheart.com/forums/index.php?showtopic=982

Slaves and Employees

Now Paul speaks to slaves[13] and masters. We just don't have slavery in our cultures of the type seen in the Mediterranean world. Sadly, there is illegally slavery where immigrants are exploited for their labor or young girls sold into the sex trade. But that's not the same as slavery in Paul's day, where up to one third of the population might be slaves. Nor can we find a helpful analogy from plantation slavery in the American South from the 1600s to the 1860s. That was cruel, repressive, and racial in nature.

Slavery in Paul's day derived primarily from three sources: prisoners of war captured in the wars of Roman conquest (largely over by the time Colossians was written), children of slaves, and those who became slaves from debt. Slavery was widespread, especially outside of Palestine. Slaves weren't free, but were considered part of the

---

[11] *Erethizō*, BDAG 391.

[12] *Athymeō*, BDAG 25.

[13] "Slaves" (NIV, NRSV), "servants" (KJV) is *doulos*, pertaining to being under someone's total control, slavish, servile, subject," here "male slave as an entity in a socioeconomic context, slave" (BDAG 260, 1a).

household. They were usually of the same race as their owners, but were often from other ethnic origin.

Since the message of the gospel appealed especially to the poor and oppressed, there were many slaves within Christian congregations.

Though slavery in Paul's day has no modern-day equivalence, I've found that many of Paul's instructions to both slaves and masters are quite applicable to relations between employers or managers and employees. Yes, employees are free to quit, while slaves weren't. And no, employers don't have absolute power over their employees – except in the workplace, perhaps. But Paul's instructions tend to apply quite well, so I'll pursue those applications as we look at this passage.

Slaves, Obey Your Masters (3:22)

Paul instructed slaves:

> "Slaves, obey your earthly masters in everything; and do it, not only when their eye is on you and to win their favor, but with sincerity of heart and reverence for the Lord." (3:22)

"Obey" (*hypakouō*) means to follow the master's instructions precisely. The obedience is to be total "in everything," specifically, in everything under the master or employer's sphere of authority. But notice that Paul qualifies this sentence. "Earthly masters," they may be, but neither slave owners or employers have ultimate authority. That is reserved exclusively to God on high. He is to be obeyed always when there is a conflict between his commands and a human master's commands.

Paul isn't just speaking of outward obedience of the letter of the command, however. He is touching on attitude.

> "... Do it, not only when their eye is on you and to win their favor, but with sincerity of heart and reverence for the Lord." (3:22b)

- **"When their eye is on you"** (NIV), "while being watched" (NRSV), "eyeservice" (KJV) is *ophthalmodoulia*, "service that is performed only to make an impression in the owner's presence, eye-service."[14]

- **"To win their favor"** (NIV), "to please them" (NRSV), "menpleasers" (KJV) is *anthrōpareskos*, "one who tries to make an impression on others, fawner, timeserv-

---

[14] *Ophthalmodoulia*, BDAG 743.

er,"[15] from *anthrōpos*, "man, human" + *areskō*, "to act in a fawning manner, win favor, please, flatter."[16]

Don't just "kiss up" to your bosses when they are present, but then slack off when they are away, says Paul. That is hypocrisy. Rather we are to obey our employers with honesty and sincerity.

- **"Sincerity"** (NIV), "wholeheartedly" (NRSV), "singleness" is *haplotēs*, literally, "singleness." In the New Testament, it is used especially of personal integrity expressed in word or action, "simplicity, sincerity, uprightness, frankness."[17] Here it is used along with "heart" (*kardia*), "a sincere heart."

- **"With reverence"** (NIV), "fearing" (NRSV, KJV) is *phobeō*, "to fear," here with the sense, "to have a profound measure of respect for, (have) reverence, respect," with special reference to fear of offending.[18] The idea here is to show respect for the master's or employer's role.

As Working for the Lord, Not Men (3:23-25)

Now Paul goes deeper into the work ethic that we should have as Christians:

"[23] Whatever you do, work at it with all your heart, as working for the Lord, not for men, [24] since you know that you will receive an inheritance from the Lord as a reward. It is the Lord Christ you are serving. [25] Anyone who does wrong will be repaid for his wrong, and there is no favoritism." (3:23-25)

There's a phrase common in some circles: "Good enough for government work." In other words, the job isn't performed with excellence, but good enough for the low standards that the government often has. For some of us, "good enough" represents our whole attitude toward life and work. But Paul suggests that our standard shouldn't be just "acceptable," but "excellence." He says:

"Whatever you do, work at it with all your heart, as working for the Lord, not for men." (3:23)

Look at the phrases:

---

[15] *Anthrōpareskos*, BDAG 80.
[16] *Areskō*, BDAG 129, 1.
[17] *Haplotēs*, BDAG 104, 1.
[18] *Phobeō*, BDAG 1061, 2a.

- **"Whatever you do."** Our goal should be excellence in any project, whether the boss is watching or not.

- **"With all your heart"** (NIV), "put yourselves into it" (NRSV), "heartily" (KJV) is made up of two words: the preposition *ek*, "out of" and *psuchē*, "soul" as the seat and center of the inner human life in its many and varied aspects. The phrase means, "from the heart, gladly."[19]

- **"As working[20] for the Lord, not for men"** (NIV). Wow! This is a radical statement. We are to consider our work as performed for God himself. This has a number of implications.

God Is Our Employer or Master

Look at the passage again:

"[23] Whatever you do, work at it with all your heart, as working for the Lord, not for men, [24] since you know that you will receive an inheritance from the Lord as a reward. It is the Lord Christ you are serving. [25] Anyone who does wrong will be repaid for his wrong, and there is no favoritism." (3:23-25)

In what sense should we consider God our employer? Paul brings out three points:

1. Jesus is our Lord of lords. Paul calls him "the Lord Christ," that is, the Messiah who is superior to all. He is Lord (*kyrios*) over our earthly lords or masters (same word, *kyrios*) or employers. We serve[21] him, answer to him, and put his interests first. In a real sense the work we do for an under-lord, we do as unto Him. He is the one whom we serve with our actions. Our place of employment may be as a household slave or the CEO of a great company, but our Lord is the same.

2. Jesus pays great wages. I know this will upset us evangelicals who have been raised on the concept of grace rather than works (Ephesians 2:8-9), but bear with me. Elsewhere Paul deliberately contrasts wages and grace (Romans 4:4; 6:23). But here Paul is using an analogy that slaves and employees can understand. The word "reward" is *antapodosis*, "that which is given to someone in exchange for what has been done, repaying, reward."[22]

---

[19] *Psuchē*, BDAG 1098, 2c.

[20] "Work at it" (NIV) is *ergazomai*, "to engage in activity that involves effort, work, be active" (BDAG 389, 1).

[21] "Serve" is *douleuō*, "to act or conduct oneself as one in total service to another, perform the duties of a slave, serve, obey" (BDAG 259, 2aβ).

[22] *Antapodosis*, BDAG 87.

We must realize, however, that in Paul's day, slaves didn't normally earn a wage. They were wholly owned by a master, who provided them room and board, usually within his own household. But he didn't owe them any wages nor did they inherit his property as would his sons.

So when Paul says to slaves that "you will receive an inheritance from the Lord as a reward," he is telling them that Jesus is a better master or Lord. He pays! The wages or recompense he offers will come in the form of our inheritance (*klēronomia*) of all of God's riches, to be received when Christ comes again. Yes, our inheritance includes salvation, but also the additional rewards and blessings that Christ chooses to bestow upon us.

If you're a slave, the idea of an inheritance is huge. If you're an employee earning a paycheck, this is huge, too. Yes, if you live in the West, you may earn a few million dollars over the course of your lifetime. But that is nothing compared to the inheritance you will receive in glory. Does it pay to serve Christ? You bet it does! And since he pays better than your earthly employer, you owe him your first allegiance. Remember, this is an analogy; don't try to push it too far.

3. Jesus is a just employer. On earth people do things behind the boss's back and get away with it. Bosses often show favoritism to their favorites. Sometimes bosses (and slave-owners) are unfair and cruel to those under them. Not so with Jesus. He is just.

> "Anyone who does wrong[23] will be repaid for his wrong, and there is no favoritism." (3:25)

How are we to take this warning about justice and favoritism? Is it directed at slaves or at masters? Probably at both, since the sentence occurs at the junction between Paul's directions for slaves and his direction for masters. "Favoritism" (NIV), "partiality" (NRSV), "respect of persons" (KJV) translates a Greek compound word that renders a Hebrew concept, *prosōpolēmpsia*, from *prosōpon*, "face" + *lambanō*, "to receive, accept," that is, "to take note of the face," to judge by the face or appearance, that is, to pay regard to one's looks or circumstances rather than to his intrinsic character."[24] God doesn't care whether a person is a slave or a master; he will hold each accountable, without treating him or her according to an earthly station in life.

What are the implications of this for employees today? I can think of just a few, though these don't exhaust the subject:

---

[23] *Adikeō*, "to act in an unjust manner, do wrong" (BDAG 20, 1).
[24] Robertson, *Word Pictures*, on Romans 2:11 and Acts 10:34.

1. **The quality of our work must be excellent.** We aren't to do what we can get away with, but give it our best. Even if our employer demands us to keep up a fast pace, we still give our best within those time constraints. We don't excuse our self for sloppy work. We shouldn't feel "entitled," because we receive a low wage for our labors. With Christ as our employer, we will be abundantly compensated!

2. **Our work is holy.** I've heard people say, "I'm just a layperson" – as if this was less worthy than a full-time Christian vocation. Or, "I'm just the pastor of a small church." Baloney! God will show no favoritism to ordained clergy – except to expect more from them since they've been given more. Your life, lived out before Christ your King, is holy in and of itself. Christ is your employer, your master – no matter what kind of work you do (or did) to earn a living. This is no small thing! You are not judged in comparison to others – that's our human way of judging.

3. **Our attitude towards God shows in our attitude towards our employer.** If you are bitter towards your employer, whom God has put over you for now, how can you give your job your best? Christ requires your attitude at work to be pleasing to him.

I'm sure that as you talk to the Lord about this, he will show you more implications of Jesus being your employer.

Q3. (Colossians 3:22-24) If you apply Paul's instructions to slaves to the role of being an employee, what is the role of sincerity as an employee? How do we live this out when working under a poor boss? In what sense are we actually "working for the Lord"? What would happen in the workplace, if we actually began to live by these attitudes of heart?

http:/www.joyfulheart.com/forums/index.php?showtopic=983

Masters, Be Fair to Your Slaves (3:25-4:1)

" [3:25] Anyone who does wrong will be repaid for his wrong, and there is no favoritism. [4:1] Masters, provide your slaves with what is right and fair, because you know that you also have a Master in heaven." (3:25-4:1)

As we observed above, verse 25 applies as much to masters and employers as it does to slaves and employees. You may be able to "get away with" some action or attitude here on earth, but not before Christ. Paul reminds human masters[25] that "you also have a Master in heaven" (4:1b). As a result of this, masters are held responsible for three things:

1. Providing for them. "Provide" (NIV), "treat" (NRSV), "give" (KJV) is *parechō*, which, in classical Greek, carries the idea, "hand over, furnish, supply, provide" for someone.[26] Masters didn't pay slaves, but they were to give them enough to eat and a place to live. Employers, too, are to provide for their employees. Often, employers think of themselves in terms of buying a person's time, as if it were a commodity, with no strings attached. Don't give them enough hours, so that you have to pay benefits, is a way of life. But hours are not a commodity; they represent people -- people whom God loves and people who pray to him. When we employ people we also take on a responsibility to help provide for their needs. Making a living is not just our employees' problem; as employers it is our responsibility as well. This casts a whole new light on the subject.

2. Providing for them what is just and right. "Right" (NIV), "just/justly" (NRSV, KJV) is *dikaios*, "obligatory in view of certain requirements of justice, right, fair, equitable."[27] Employers aren't just to pay as little as the market will bear. We will be judged by our Master in terms of what is just and right, not just by market conditions. Is it just, is it right to employ laborers in sweatshop conditions and pay them a pittance? God will hold us employers responsible for what we do.

3. Providing for them what is fair. "Fair/fairly" (NIV, NRSV), "equal" (KJV) is *isotēs*. The root idea of the word is "equality," as in 2 Corinthians 8:13-14. Here it carries the extended idea of "state of being fair, fairness."[28] Paul wasn't a social reformer pressing for absolute equality of earthly station and condition. But the implications of his

---

[25] "Masters" is *kyrios*, "one who is in charge by virtue of possession, owner" (BDAG 572, II1b).

[26] *Parechō*, Liddell-Scott, A; cf. "grant something to someone" (BDAG 776, 3b).

[27] *Dikaios*, BDAG 247, 2.

[28] *Isotēs*, BDAG 483, 2; also Liddell-Scott, III. "fair dealing, impartiality."

teaching is clearly that masters and slaves are equal before God, and masters must not forget it. In Ephesians, Paul reminds us:

"The Lord will reward everyone for whatever good he does, whether he is slave or free." (Ephesians 6:8)

We are equal before God. It is from this foundation in Christianity that the U.S. Declaration of Independence would later declare the radical contention (for its time):

"We hold these truths to be self-evident, that all men are created equal, that they are endowed by their Creator with certain unalienable Rights...."

The Gospel sets people free as its truth and the implications of its truth are worked throughout a culture. When the Declaration of Independence was written in 1776, slaves were not free in the fledgling country. But because of the truth of the Biblical principle of the equality of all before God, Abraham Lincoln issued the Emancipation Proclamation freeing slaves (1863), which would become part of the U.S. Constitution in the Thirteenth Amendment outlawing slavery and involuntary servitude.

Churches, Be Fair to Your Church Employees

You may not be an employer, but in a sense, if you are a member of a church – and especially if you are a church leader – then you are responsible for how your pastor and church employees are paid. Do you pay the least you can? Do you take pride in keeping your pastor or church employees poor? Are you fair in your dealings?

God will hold us all responsible for carrying out our roles where he has put us. There is no partiality. He holds us all responsible.

Q4. (Colossians 3:25-4:1) What instructions does Paul give masters – or employers, in our culture? What would happen in the workplace if employers sought to live by this rule?
http:/www.joyfulheart.com/forums/index.php?showtopic=984

Paul's desire in Colossians 3 is to help Christian believers to begin to shine with the light of Christ – in their personal characters and in their homes and workplaces. Christ, through Paul, is seeking for us to experience "the peace of Christ" ruling in our hearts and homes.

Prayer

Father, sometimes we try to look good for church people, but at home and at work we hardly act like disciples of Jesus. Forgive us. Work in our hearts and attitudes so that we might reflect your glory in our homes and offices and shops. Grant it, O God. In Jesus' name, we pray. Amen.

Key Verse

Whatever you do, work at it with all your heart, as working for the Lord, not for men, since you know that you will receive an inheritance from the Lord as a reward. It is the Lord Christ you are serving. (Colossians 3:23-24, NIV)

8. Final Instructions and Greetings (Colossians 4:2-18)

Paul concludes his letter to the Colossians with instructions on prayer and witnessing, as well as personal notes and greetings.

Devote Yourselves to Prayer (4:2)

First, some words on prayer. This isn't a carefully outlined teaching, just the brief encouragements that come to the apostle's mind as he writes to the church.

> "Devote yourselves to prayer, being watchful and thankful." (4:2)

Perhaps their praying has been ragged and hit and miss. Paul gives three characteristics in prayer that they need to work on:

1. Persistence. "Devote" (NIV, NRSV), "continue in" (KJV) is *proskartereō*, "to persist in something," here, "busy oneself

Francisco de Goya y Lucientes, "St. Peter Repentant" (1823-25), oil on canvas, 29 x 25.5 cm, Phillips Collection, Washington

with, be busily engaged in, be devoted to,"[1] from *pros*, "on, at" + *kartereō*, "be steadfast, endure." It's easy to skip times of prayer, to rush over our devotional time because we're so busy. Also, we have a spiritual enemy who tries to distract us from talking to God. But Paul highlights prayer's importance: persist in prayer, be devoted to it!

2. Alertness. "Being watchful" (NIV), "keeping alert" (NRSV), "watch" (KJV) is *grēgoreō*, "to stay awake, be watchful," then figuratively as here, "to be in constant readiness, be on the alert."[2] The verb comes from *egrēgora*, "to have been roused from sleep, to be awake," the perfect of *egeirō*, "wake, arouse" someone from sleep. Have your prayers ever put you to sleep? Mine have. We can go through the motions of prayer

---

[1] *Proskartereō*, BDAG 883, 2a.
[2] *Grēgoreō*, BDAG 208, 2.

without having our minds in gear. Paul urges attention to what we're doing. This is not just a mindless exercise. It is communication with the Most High God.

3. Thankfulness. "Being thankful" (NIV), "thanksgiving" (NRSV, KJV) is *eucharistia*, "the expression or content of gratitude, the rendering of thanks, thanksgiving," from which we get our English word "Eucharist."[3] Prayer is not just petitioning God to do this or that. It is communication with a person. Prayer includes thankfulness, which is the language of faith. When we thank God for what he has done, it encourages us in faith to expect answers to our other prayers.

Q1. (Colossians 4:2) What guidelines does Paul give us to form our praying habits? If you put these into practice fully, how would they affect your prayer life? What problems would they help correct?
http://www.joyfulheart.com/forums/index.php?showtopic=985

Paul Requests Prayer for His Ministry Team (4:3-4)

Now Paul asks for specific prayers to be made for him.

"[3] And pray for us, too, that God may open a door for our message, so that we may proclaim the mystery of Christ, for which I am in chains. [4] Pray that I may proclaim it clearly, as I should." (4:3-4)

Notice that Paul doesn't ask prayer for just himself. He sees himself as part of a ministry team – even while in jail in Rome. Along with Paul are his co-worker Timothy (1:1) and others, including his fellow prisoner Aristarchus (4:10a), Mark (4:10b), Jesus Justus (4:11), Epaphras (4:12), Luke (4:14a), and Demas (4:14b). Some were well-trained workers by now, able to minister independently. Others, Paul probably had with him to train for future ministry. Paul asks prayer for the whole team.

Prayer for Success of the Mission (4:3-4)

Paul has two primary requests:

---

[3] *Eucharistia*, BDAG 416, 2. The word is also found at 2:7.

1. That God will provide opportunities to speak the Word.

2. That God will help them proclaim the Word with clarity.

Prayer for an Open Door (4:3)

Paul's first request is for an open door:

> "And pray for us, too, that God may open a door for our message, so that we may proclaim the mystery of Christ, for which I am in chains." (4:3)

This figure of an open door signifying opportunity occurs several other times in the New Testament.

> [Paul and Barnabas] "reported all that God had done through them and how he had **opened the door of faith** to the Gentiles." (Acts 14:27)

> "But I will stay on at Ephesus until Pentecost, because **a great door for effective work has opened** to me...." (1 Corinthians 16:8-9)

> "I went to Troas to preach the gospel of Christ and found that the Lord had **opened a door** for me." (2 Corinthians 2:12)

> [To the church in Philadelphia]: "See, I **have placed before you an open door** that no one can shut." (Revelation 3:8)

Jesus himself used this terminology as he instructed his disciples about prayer:

> "So I say to you: Ask and it will be given to you; seek and you will find; knock and the door will be opened to you.... To him who knocks, the door will be opened." (Luke 11:9-10)

"Pray," Paul says, "that God may open a door for our message[4]" (4:3). Have you ever had a time when you couldn't seem to find a handle on a situation, a place to start on a project, a strategy for evangelism? Do you seem to be beating your head against a wall with no effect?

Sometimes we have no opportunities because of our laziness. But Paul – even in prison[5] – was anything but lazy! Unless God creates an opportunity, we are ineffective. When God opens the door of opportunity, we need to be ready to step through it.

---

[4] "Message" (NIV), "word" (NRSV), "utterance" (KJV) is *logos*.

[5] "Chains" (NIV), "prison" (NRSV), "bonds" (KJV) is *deō*, "to confine a person or thing by various kinds of restraints, bind, tie." (BDAG 222, 1b).

How often do you ask others to pray for you that you may have an opportunity to witness at work, to say a word to a loved one about Christ? This kind of prayer should be often on our lips and God is able to answer it.

Prayer for Clarity of Speech (4:4)

Paul isn't asking prayer for a preaching opportunity. That's a different Greek word. Here he seems to be asking for an opportunity to speak personally – perhaps to Caesar's representative, or the Praetorian Guard, or to his keepers.

"Pray that I may proclaim it clearly, as I should." (4:4)

"Proclaim clearly" (NIV), "reveal clearly" (NRSV), "make manifest" (KJV) translate two words: *laleō*, the most common word for "say, speak"[6] and *phaneroō* (which we've seen before with regard to Christ being revealed), "to cause to become known, disclose, show, make known."[7]

So Paul's request for prayer while he is in prison is not for his welfare, but for effectiveness in personal ministry. Send an opportunity, O Lord. Then when you provide it, let me speak with such clarity that the message will be communicated. He is talking about everyday evangelism.

Q2. (Colossians 4:3-4) What prayer request does Paul ask of the Colossian believers? What does it mean to pray for an "open door." Why does he ask for prayer in communicating the gospel? Isn't he an "old hand" at this? Why does he need help?
http://www.joyfulheart.com/forums/index.php?showtopic=986

Wisdom Toward Outsiders (4:5-6)

Now he speaks to the Colossian believers about their everyday evangelism.

---

[6] *Laleō*, BDAG 582, 2b.
[7] *Phaneroō*, BDAG 1048, 2aα.

"⁵ Be wise in the way you act toward outsiders; make the most of every opportunity.
⁶ Let your conversation be always full of grace, seasoned with salt, so that you may know how to answer everyone." (4:5-6)

The outsiders that Paul is referring to are those who are outside the community of Christian believers. The way we act or conduct ourselves[8] with non-Christians is important. We need to be wise and loving.

You've probably seen Christians act in outrageous ways around unbelievers, in ways that might make you want to crawl in a hole and disappear. That is why Paul calls for practical wisdom.[9] Sometimes we're so embarrassed by the behavior of fellow Christians that we bend the other way and remain completely silent. That isn't the answer, says Paul.

Instead, we are literally to "redeem the time" (KJV). What does that mean? The phrase uses two words.

- **"Opportunity"** (NIV), "time" (KJV, NRSV) is *kairos,* a word that carries the idea here of "favorable time, opportunity."[10]

- **"Make the most of"** (NIV, NRSV), "redeeming" (KJV) is *exagorazō.* The basic meaning is "deliver, liberate," but a figurative sense used here is "to gain something," especially advantage or opportunity, "make the most of."[11]

So Paul tells us to take full advantage of every opportunity we are given. In Ephesians a similar exhortation is followed by a reason: "because the days are evil" (Ephesians 5:16).

Guidelines for Conversations with Non-Christians (4:6)

We can't afford to miss opportunities to speak an effective word for Christ in our everyday conversation[12] with non-Christians when the opportunity presents itself.

"Let your conversation be always full of grace, seasoned with salt, so that you may know how to answer everyone." (4:6)

---

[8] "Act" (NIV), conduct (NRSV), "walk" (KJV) is *peripateō,* literally, "to walk about," then, by extension, "to conduct one's life, comport oneself, behave, live as habit of conduct" (BDAG 803, 2aα).

[9] *Sophia,* "the capacity to understand and function accordingly, wisdom" (BDAG 934, 1bα).

[10] *Kairos* means "a point of time or period of time, time, period" frequently with implication of being especially fit for something, here "a moment or period as especially appropriate, the right, proper, favorable time" or "opportunity." (BDAG 497, 1b). The other primary Greek word for time is *chronos,* from which we get our English word "chronology," is used more to express sequential or chronological time.

[11] *Exagorazō,* BDAG 343, 2.

[12] "Conversation" (NIV), "speech" (NRSV, KJV) is *logos,* "word, of utterance, chiefly oral" (BDAG 599, 1a).

"Full of grace" (NIV), "gracious" (NRSV), "grace" (KJV) is the key concept underlying our conversations. "Grace" (*charis*) is used commonly by Paul to express the free gift of salvation through Christ, since the basic meaning of *charis* is "favor" that is expressed by the giver of his own will, without any need for the recipient to respond in kind, that is, undeserved favor. But in this context, *charis* has a widely used meaning in common Greek, "a winning quality or attractiveness that invites a favorable reaction, graciousness, attractiveness, charm, winsomeness." For example, the same word is used in Luke 4:22 to describe Jesus' "gracious words."

To understand what this is, contrast loving, open, friendly speech with an attitude and words that are perceived by non-Christian neighbors as being:

• Defensive	• Hard
• Condescending	• Legalistic
• Holier-than-thou	• Critical
• Cold	• Naïve
• Manipulative	• Pushy
• Negative	• Uncaring

You know what I mean. So often the worldly caricature of "born again" Christians is negative. In films and television, Christians aren't often portrayed as loving, open, caring people, as would be required by Paul's expression "full of grace" or "gracious." Why? Partly because we're in a spiritual warfare in which Satan is seeking to poison people's minds against Christians. But partly because we haven't learned to be gracious and loving.

Next we find the phrase "seasoned with salt." In the Sermon on the Mount, Jesus used the figure of saltiness in the context of witness (Matthew 5:13). He's not talking about salt's use as a preservative there, but its tastiness, its flavorfulness, the way it gives just the right added flavor and tang to food to make it exquisite to the palate.[13]

The NASB translates this verse, "with grace, *as though* seasoned with salt," making "seasoned with salt," as an explanation of full of grace rather than a different quality altogether. It's very possible that this is Paul's meaning.

---

[13] For a deeper explanation of Jesus' use of the figure of salt, see my exposition of Matthew 5:13 in *Sermon on the Mount: The Jesus Manifesto* (JesusWalk Publications, 2008).

Grace and love *are* the unique tang of our testimony, if we're following Jesus. So often we try to blend in with a tasteless and insipid world. No! We have a unique flavor of grace that the world needs – and is desperate for, if they can recognize it as genuine and not self-serving.

Paul's instruction concludes with the phrase, "so that you may know how to answer everyone." Peter said it this way:

> "Always be prepared to give an answer to everyone who asks you to give the reason for the hope that you have. But do this with gentleness and respect...." (1 Peter 3:15)

We'd like, of course, to be able to answer questions about Christianity with a thorough knowledge of the Bible, to stun our critics by the force of our logic and our preparation through apologetics courses to field any question.

But the point of Paul's and Peter's counsel to us is two-fold:

1. Willingness to seize the opportunities God gives; don't be silent.

2. Be gracious and gentle in your reply.

That is what we all *can* do, from the youngest Christian to the most mature believer. And that is what we *must* do to serve Christ as his witnesses here on earth.

Q3. (Colossians 4:5-6) What instructions does Paul give us in sharing our faith with non-believers? Why, do you think, we sometimes let opportunities slip by? How will our conversation being "full of grace" help us represent Christ well?
http:/www.joyfulheart.com/forums/index.php?showtopic=987

Tychicus and Onesimus (4:7-8)

Now Paul turns from practical teaching to personal comments, as he winds down his letter. First is Tychicus.[14] He was Paul's traveling companion on several occasions, and later a person whom Paul could send as his representative to troubleshoot problems in the various churches (Acts 20:4; Ephesus 6:21; 2 Timothy 4:12; Titus 3:12).

---

[14] His name means "fortunate," from *tugchano*, "to happen, to fall out."

> "[7] Tychicus will tell you all the news about me. He is a dear brother, a faithful minister and fellow servant in the Lord. [8] I am sending him to you for the express purpose that you may know about our circumstances and that he may encourage your hearts." (4:7-8)

These words are very similar to Paul's comments at the end of his Letter to the Ephesians. Ephesus, remember, is about 100 miles west of Colossae, the large capital city on the west coast of Asia Minor. It is likely that Tychicus will carry letters to both Ephesus and Colossae at the same time – or come soon after – to represent Paul personally in both churches. Notice Paul's description of him in verse 7:

1. Dear brother

2. Faithful minister (*diakonos*, "minister, servant")

3. Fellow servant in the Lord (*sundoulos*, "fellow-slave")

Tychicus isn't commended as a great speaker or a fiery evangelist, but one who is faithful and reliable, a good solid co-worker upon whom Paul could rely, who was committed to the mission. Do you have this quality of faithfulness?

His mission is two-fold:

1. **Relay information**, "that you may know about our circumstances," thus building both prayer and financial support.

2. **Encouragement**, "that he may encourage your hearts."

This sounds like the purpose of many missionary presentations in our own day. Sometimes our congregations can become isolated from the "front lines." It's vital that we stay in touch – and be touched by – Christ's work around the world.

Onesimus (4:9)

> "He is coming with Onesimus, our faithful and dear brother, who is one of you. They will tell you everything that is happening here." (4:9)

Onesimus,[15] we'll learn as we study the brief Letter to Philemon, is a runaway slave who has met Paul in Rome, become a Christian, and is now returning to his master, Philemon, in hopes of being freed.

---

[15] Onesimus means "profitable," from *oninemi*, "to have the benefit of, enjoy."

Aristarchus, Mark and Jesus Justus (4:10-11)

> [10] My fellow prisoner Aristarchus sends you his greetings, as does Mark, the cousin of Barnabas. (You have received instructions about him; if he comes to you, welcome him.) [11] Jesus, who is called Justus, also sends greetings. These are the only Jews among my fellow workers for the kingdom of God, and they have proved a comfort to me." (4:10-11)

Aristarchus is one of Paul's travel companions, a Jewish-Christian Macedonian from Thessalonica (Acts 19:29; 20:4; 27:2; Philemon 24). He is currently in Rome in prison as is Paul. It is clear, however, that Paul is able to communicate with him regularly. They may even be staying together, guarded by the same guard.

John Mark is also with Paul in Rome at this time. He had gone on Paul's first missionary journey with Barnabas, but had left early. As he planned his second trip, Paul wasn't eager to include him, causing Mark and his cousin Barnabas to set out on their own missionary trip to Cyprus (Acts 12:12, 25; 15:37-39; 2 Timothy 4:11; Philemon 24). But the rift has healed and Paul has left instructions to the churches to receive Mark openly.

Mark was also an associate of Peter, who may have been in prison in Rome about the very same time as Paul. According to Irenaeus (died 202 AD), after Peter's and Paul's deaths in Rome, "... Mark, the disciple and interpreter of Peter, did also hand down to us in writing what had been preached by Peter,"[16] that is, the Gospel of Mark.

"Jesus, who is called Justus," also Jewish, is mentioned only here in the Bible.

Epaphras (4:12-13)

> "[12] Epaphras, who is one of you and a servant of Christ Jesus, sends greetings. He is always wrestling in prayer for you, that you may stand firm in all the will of God, mature and fully assured. [13] I vouch for him that he is working hard for you and for those at Laodicea and Hierapolis." (4:12-13)

Epaphras, you'll remember from the Introduction and Lesson 1 (1:7-8), is probably the founder of the Church in Colossae. He has gone to Rome to seek out Paul and ask him to write a letter to the Colossians to help the believers understand how they are being deceived by the false teachers. In Lesson 1 we examined four characteristics of his character and ministry: beloved, a fellow-servant or fellow-slave of Christ, faithful, and a "minister of Christ."

---

[16] Irenaeus, *Against Heresies*, 3,1,1.

In his letter to Philemon, Paul speaks of Epaphras as "my fellow prisoner in Christ Jesus" (Philemon 1:23), so apparently he is incarcerated at this time with Paul – on what charge we do not know.

What we learn new about Epaphras in this passage is that he "is always wrestling in prayer for you." This term "wrestling" (NIV, NRSV), "laboring fervently" (KJV) is *agōnizomai* (related to the noun *agōn* which we saw in 1:7). The basic idea is "to engage in an athletic contest." Here the word is used figuratively, generally "to fight, struggle."[17]

This teaches us that intercessory prayer is not easy. It is "labor intensive," as Paul says that Epaphras is "working hard" (4:13) for the readers. The phrase is literally "he has much labor," employing the noun *ponos*, "work that involves much exertion or trouble, (hard) labor, toil." The word can also imply the experience of great trouble on account of his prayers.[18] Since intercessory prayer is spiritual warfare of a rather intense nature, it can be draining. The ministry of intercessory prayer is behind the scenes, but of vital importance for the health and success of the church's ministry.

Notice that Epaphras is praying for three churches, clustered within a few miles of each other: Colossae, Laodicea, and Hierapolis.[19] These churches were closely tied both geographically and in ministry.

Luke and Demas (4:14)

"Our dear friend Luke, the doctor, and Demas send greetings." (4:14)

Paul's companion during his imprisonment is Luke, "the beloved physician," who had travelled extensively with him. Paul refers to him as a "fellow-worker" in Philemon 24. He was with Paul at the end of his life (2 Timothy 4:11).

Luke[20] wrote both the Gospel of Luke and the Acts of the Apostles, almost one quarter of the New Testament. Apparently, he was a Gentile, since he is spoken of separately from those with Paul at Rome who were Jews (4:11). According to the *Anti-Marcionite Prologue to the Gospel of Luke* (perhaps from the late second century AD), we learn that:

"Luke is a Syrian of Antioch, a Syrian by race, a physician by profession. He had become a disciple of the apostles and later followed Paul until his (Paul's) martyr-

---

[17] *Agōnizomai*, BDAG 17, 2b.
[18] *Ponos*, BDAG 852, 1, from *penomai*, "to toil."
[19] For their location, see the map in the Introduction.
[20] Luke is contracted from Latin *Lucanus*.

dom, having served the Lord continuously, unmarried, without children, filled with the Holy Spirit he died at the age of eighty-four years in Boeotia."[21]

Demas[22] was another of Paul's close associates, mentioned here and in Philemon 24. But, sadly, he was not with Paul at the end. Paul writes:

> "Do your best to come to me quickly, for Demas, because he loved this world, has deserted me and has gone to Thessalonica." (2 Timothy 4:9-10)

Greetings to the Church at Laodicea (4:15-16)

Laodicea was about 12 miles west of Colossae, larger and more important. Paul has also written them a letter, which, unfortunately, has not survived.

> "[15] Give my greetings to the brothers at Laodicea, and to Nympha and the church in her house. [16] After this letter has been read to you, see that it is also read in the church of the Laodiceans and that you in turn read the letter from Laodicea." (4:15-16)

Greek *Nymphan*[23] could refer to either a male or female resident of Laodicea, since the preposition "their" or "her" has different readings in ancient texts.[24]

Notice the reference to "the church in her house" (4:15). Up until the third century the church didn't normally have buildings dedicated to public worship. Rather, they met in homes, usually the larger homes of the wealthier members of the church (Philemon 2; Romans 16:5; 1 Corinthians 16:19; and Acts 12:12). For us to imagine that a *bigger* church is a *better* church is a modern phenomenon. In ancient times a large church in a city would be distributed among many house churches, with multiple elders presiding over the various parts of the flock (see Acts 20:17-35; 11:30; 14:23; 15:4; 16:4; 1 Timothy 15:7; Titus 1:5; James 5:14; 1 Peter 5:1).

---

[21] Cited by Helmut Koester, *Ancient Christian Gospels: Their History and Development* (Harrisburg, PA. Trinity Press International. 1990), p. 335.

[22] Demas is probably a contraction of Demetrius.

[23] A nymph in Greek mythology is a female spirit typically associated with a particular location or landform. The word was used in both male and female names of the time.

[24] Metzger prefers the feminine gender based on external texts, giving it a {C} or "considerable degree of doubt" rating (*Textual Commentary*, p. 627).

Command to Archippus (4:17)

Now Paul singles out Archippus for an exhortation. From Philemon we learn that Archippus was a leader in the church at Colossae – Paul calls him "our fellow soldier." Perhaps he is the son of Philemon and Apphia (Philemon 1-2). Here is Paul's word:

> "Tell Archippus: 'See to it that you complete the work you have received in the Lord.'" (4:17)

"See to it" (NIV), "see" (NRSV), "take heed" (KJV) is *blepō*, "to see," here with the connotation, "to pay especially close attention to something, notice, mark something." When used in the imperative, as here, it sometimes means "beware" or "look to."[25] "Work" (NIV), "task" (NRSV), "ministry" (KJV) is *diakonia*, "service," here "functioning in the interest of a larger public, service, office,"[26] perhaps "assignment." "Complete" (NIV, NRSV), "fulfill" (KJV) is *plēroō*, "fill," here, "to bring to a designed end, fulfill."[27]

I fear that there are many in our churches whom God has called to particular ministries – either formal ministries or informal ones within the congregation or in the community – who have gotten sidetracked. For one reason or another they haven't fulfilled the responsibility or call that God has placed on them. As a result, ministry is going undone, people are going uncared for, work is neglected, and the ministry of Christ on earth is lacking.

Is that you to whom God is speaking in this verse? If so, do what God has called you to do. Perhaps you can't fulfill it as you might have years ago, but do what you can now. God is patiently, tenderly, lovingly, longingly speaking to you.

Q4. (Colossians 4:17) Why do you think Archippus was singled out in verse 17? If you could invent a story of his role in the Colossian church, how would you describe Archippus? In what ways does he remind you of yourself?

http:/www.joyfulheart.com/forums/index.php?showtopic=988

Remember My Chains (4:18)

Paul concludes with three simple sentences:

---

[25] *Blepō*, BDAG 179, 4; Thayer, 2.
[26] *Diakonia*, BDAG 230, 3.
[27] *plēroō*, BDAG 828, 4b.

"I, Paul, write this greeting in my own hand. Remember my chains. Grace be with you." (4:18)

First, he assures them that the letter is authentic. Though a trained scribe probably wrote the bulk of Paul's letters, the last few lines were written in his own hand to show his readers that he indeed wrote it (1 Corinthians 16:21; Galatians 6:11; 2 Thessalonians 3:17; Philemon 19).

Next, he calls on them to "remember my chains." He is reminding them to pray for him – that is how the verb is used elsewhere (1 Thessalonians 1:3; Hebrews 13:7, etc.).

Finally he offers them a word of grace, a "grace wish," that was common at the close of his letters -- also found in secular letters. But while secular letters might ask the favor of the gods, Paul is invoking the grace of the Lord Jesus Christ that brought forgiveness where judgment was deserved, reconciliation where alienation was expected, and life where death had been the sentence. Paul expresses God's wish for you, too: "Grace – God's rich, full, free grace be with you!" Amen.

Prayer

Thank you for your grace, O Lord. You are so good to us. Thank you also for the faithful people of God who have been obedient to you, and in spite of suffering, deprivation, and death, have preserved the gospel for us, and shared it and taught it to each one of us. Thank you! In Jesus' name, we pray. Amen.

Key Verses

"Devote yourselves to prayer, being watchful and thankful." (Colossians 4:2, NIV)

"Be wise in the way you act toward outsiders; make the most of every opportunity. Let your conversation be always full of grace, seasoned with salt, so that you may know how to answer everyone." (Colossians 4:5-6, NIV)

"Tell Archippus: 'See to it that you complete the work you have received in the Lord.'" (Colossians 4:17, NIV)

9. Paul's Letter to Philemon

If you blink, you may miss Philemon (the last of the Pauline Epistles), only 25 verses long, tucked between Titus and Hebrews (the first of the General Epistles). Unlike most of Paul's letters, it is addressed to an individual, not primarily to a church. Luther saw it as:

Introduction to Philemon

We won't spend much time on the letters date and place of writing. It has been generally acknowledged as having been written by St. Paul, and seems to have been written at the same time (about 60-62 AD) and from the same

"Apostle Onesimus," mosaic (1867), St. Petka Chapel, Belgrade. Onesimus' later life is explained by several traditions, see text below.

place (in prison in Rome) as Colossians.[1] In fact, Tychicus who is carrying Paul's Letter to the Colossians to its destination, is also carrying this personal letter to Philemon, who probably lives in Colossae.

As the letter unfolds, we find that the purpose of the letter is to help reconcile Onesimus, a slave, to his master, Philemon. Since Paul bends over backwards not to tell Philemon what to do, it's difficult to learn conclusively what the difficulty is. But the two prevailing theories are:

1. **Runaway slave theory**. Onesimus is a runaway slave who has found Paul in Rome, become a Christian, and whom Paul is sending back to his master Philemon.

2. **Mediation theory**. Onesimus is a slave who has a dispute with his master Philemon, and has come to Paul to mediate in the dispute between master and slave.[2]

But the first option, that Onesimus is a runaway slave, seems to fit the facts the best, is the most popular interpretation, and is the one I am adopting in my exposition. The

---

[1] For details, see the Introduction to Colossians above.
[2] For more on theories of the purpose of the letter, see Moo, *Colossians and Philemon*, pp. 364-369.

unanswered question is how does Onesimus hook up with Paul, who is in prison in Rome, since Colossae is nearly 1,000 miles east of Rome and many weeks journey away.

We could say more, but since this is a short letter, we'll just observe as we go through the verses. There are no chapter divisions in this letter.

Greetings (verses 1-3)

"¹ Paul, a prisoner of Christ Jesus, and Timothy our brother,

to Philemon our dear friend and fellow worker, ² to Apphia our sister, to Archippus our fellow soldier and to the church that meets in your home:

³ Grace to you and peace from God our Father and the Lord Jesus Christ." (1-3)

The first few verses follow much the same "epistle format" that we observed in Colossians. Notice that there are four actual addressees:

1. **Philemon**, pastor of a house church, whom Paul recognizes as "a good friend and fellow worker." Philemon is not just a church member, but a leader – and wealthy enough to own slaves. According to letters we have from this era, we recognize that Philemon is the primary addressee, since he appears first in the list.

2. **Apphia** is likely to be Philemon's wife. If so, Paul's letter about a slave affects her household, too. But she may be a prominent member in the church. We don't know.

3. **Archippus** may well be Philemon's son, though we don't know that either. He was in active ministry in the church, since he is addressed as "fellow soldier," a term Paul has only applied elsewhere to Epaphroditus, whom he calls "my brother, fellow worker and fellow soldier" (Philippians 2:25). Note that at the end of Colossians, Paul exhorts Archippus by name: "Tell Archippus: 'See to it that you complete the work you have received in the Lord'" (Colossians 4:17).

4. **The church** that meets in your home.

Encouragement to Philemon (verses 4-7)

First, Paul writes words of encouragement to Philemon. Some see this rather cynically as "buttering him up" before he makes an appeal for Onesimus. But I don't think that's necessary. Paul is gracious in his letters, and such graciousness early in a letter is part of letter-writing etiquette in the first century.

"4 I always thank my God as I remember you in my prayers, 5 because I hear about your faith in the Lord Jesus and your love for all the saints. 6 I pray that you may be active in sharing your faith, so that you will have a full understanding of every good thing we have in Christ. 7 Your love has given me great joy and encouragement, because you, brother, have refreshed the hearts of the saints." (Philemon 4-7)

As in the beginning of Colossians, Paul enumerates the reasons that he thanks God for him in his prayers:

1. Faith in the Lord Jesus, and

2. Love for all the saints. In fact, Philemon has gone overboard in his hospitality, giving Paul "great joy and encouragement" and because he has "refreshed[3] the hearts of the saints," that is, opened his home to passing Christian workers and provided generously for their needs and their comfort.

Paul's Prayer for Philemon (verse 6)

Notice Paul's brief prayer for Philemon:

"I pray that you may be active[4] in sharing your faith, so that you will have a full understanding of every good thing we have in Christ." (verse 6)

This is a difficult sentence to translate exactly. However, "sharing" (NIV), "communication of" (KJV) is koinōnia, "participation, sharing in something."[5] But "sharing your faith" isn't the same as our present-day evangelical idiom for evangelizing a person or giving our testimony of how Christ helped us. Verse 6 is difficult to interpret precisely, but Moo paraphrases it thus:

"Philemon, I am praying that the mutual participation that arises from your faith in Christ might become effective in leading you to understand and put into practice all the good that God wills for us and that is found in our community; and do all this for the sake of Christ."

Paul's Appeal on Behalf of Onesimus (verses 8-13)

Now we come to the core of Paul's appeal on behalf of Onesimus.

---

[3] "Refreshed" is anapauō, "cause to rest, give (someone) rest, refresh, revive" (BDAG 69, 1).

[4] "Active" (NIV), "effective" (NRSV), "effectual" (KJV) is energēs, "pertaining to practical expression of capability, effective, active, powerful" (BDAG 335).

[5] Koinōnia, BDAG 553, 4. Danker translates this clause as a prayer "that your participation in the faith may be made known through your deeds."

"[8] Therefore, although in Christ I could be bold and order you to do what you ought to do, [9] yet I appeal to you on the basis of love. I then, as Paul – an old man and now also a prisoner of Christ Jesus – [10] I appeal to you for my son Onesimus, who became my son while I was in chains. [11] Formerly he was useless to you, but now he has become useful both to you and to me. [12] I am sending him – who is my very heart – back to you. [13] I would have liked to keep him with me so that he could take your place in helping me while I am in chains for the gospel." (Philemon 8-13)

Q1. (Philemon 12) Why does Paul send Onesimus back to Philemon where he can lose his freedom again? Why is it necessary for Paul to do this? Why is it necessary for Onesimus to do this?

http:/www.joyfulheart.com/forums/index.php?showtopic=989

Paul works up to his appeal – which he never quite spells out in detail – with various inducements to Philemon. He wants Philemon to act without being forced to – exactly. Paul appeals:

1. **On the basis of apostolic authority**. Paul could "be bold and order[6] you" (verse 8) – but doesn't. He only suggests that he could, if he wanted to.

2. **On the basis of love** (verse 9a). Paul has recalled instances of Philemon's love that have reached Paul's ears, so he appeals to Philemon as one would to a brother who is rich in love.

3. **On the basis of respect for Paul's age** (verse 9b). In our culture, age is looked down upon. But in Paul's world, age was considered worthy of great respect. The old were deemed to be wise.

---

[6] "Order" (NIV, NRSV), "enjoin" (KJV) is *epitassō*, "to command with authority, order, command someone" (BDAG 383).

4. **On the basis of honoring Paul's sufferings.** In verses 9c and 13b, Paul reminds Philemon that he is suffering in prison for the sake of the gospel even as he writes this appeal.

5. **On the basis of Paul's spiritual fatherhood of Onesimus** (verse 10). Paul apparently led Onesimus to Christ while they were together. He "became my son while I was in chains," says Paul.

6. **On the basis of Onesimus's usefulness to Paul's** (verse 11). Onesimus was useful to Paul and served him while in prison, probably by attending to his personal needs, perhaps shopping, carrying messages, etc. I need him, Paul says, "while I am in chains for the gospel" (verse 13b). Don't miss the play on words here. "Onesimus" means in Greek, "profitable, helpful," from *onēsis*, "profit," and therefore is a common name given slaves.[7] Previously, when Onesimus had been a slave in Philemon's household, as yet not a Christian, he was pretty worthless. The word is *achrēstos*, "pertaining to not serving any beneficial purpose, useless, worthless."[8] But now Onesimus ("profitable one") is *euchrēstos*, "pertaining to being helpful or beneficial, useful, serviceable,"[9] that is, he now is fulfilling his name, which means "profitable, helpful one."

7. **On the basis of Paul's affection for Onesimus.** Paul says that Onesimus "is my very heart" (verse 12), "he is very dear to me" (verse 16).

8. **On the basis of Philemon's debt to Paul.** Paul says, "I would have liked to keep him with me so that he could take your place in helping me while I am in chains for the gospel" (verse 13). Later he notes, "not to mention that you owe me your very self" (verse 19b). Paul was the one who had led Philemon to the Lord.

It is a very strong appeal. How can Philemon resist?

Respect for Philemon's Will (verse 14)

Paul makes a strong appeal indeed, but he seeks Philemon's action out of his own free will rather than in response to an apostolic command. God always seeks our heart rather than merely our robotic response.

---

[7] Lightfoot, *Colossians and Philemon*, p. 310.
[8] *Achrēstos*, BDAG 160.
[9] *Euchrēstos*, BDAG 413.

> "But I did not want to do anything without your consent, so that any favor you do will be spontaneous and not forced." (verse 14)

Does Paul go over the top in supporting his plea. He's near the edge, perhaps, but yet he seeks Philemon's heart decision. That's why he doesn't go farther and command Philemon.

Q2. (Philemon 14) Why doesn't Paul come right out and command Philemon? Is this out of respect for his personhood or to build moral character in him -- or what?
http:/www.joyfulheart.com/forums/index.php?showtopic=990

A New Relationship (verses 15-16)

Paul is now reasoning with Philemon, reflecting with him on the wonder of Christian fellowship.

> "[15] Perhaps the reason he was separated from you for a little while was that you might have him back for good – [16] no longer as a slave, but better than a slave, as a dear brother. He is very dear to me but even dearer to you, both as a man and as a brother in the Lord." (verses 15-16)

Previously, when Onesimus had been a house slave, he had been unconverted, and by all accounts pretty worthless. Perhaps he had even stolen from Philemon as he had run away (verse 18). But his running away was ultimately for the best. Probably Philemon had prayed for his salvation, as he would have for each member of his household. Now God has answered his prayers. Strange, how God can turn what is intended as evil against us into good (Genesis 50:20; Romans 8:28).

Now that he has become a Christian, Onesimus is more than a slave. He is a brother. Once he was considered a person of a lower class, and perhaps looked down on as a poor slave at that. Now he can be considered as one who is truly "dear." The word is *agapētos*, pertaining to one who is dearly loved, dear, beloved, prized, valued."[10]

---

[10] *Agapētos*, BDAG 7, 2.

I am sure that Philemon is struggling with this. He has resented Onesimus for months, perhaps years, for running away and depriving him of the labor that he legally has a right to in that culture. And now Paul says that Onesimus is to be considered as one who is "beloved," a brother. Hmmm. Sometimes God needs to stretch us so we can see beyond our prejudices.

The Appeal: Welcome Him (verses 17-21)

After all this introduction, Paul comes to his point. He asks that Philemon "welcome" Onesimus.

> [17] So if you consider me a partner, welcome him as you would welcome me. [18] If he has done you any wrong or owes you anything, charge it to me. [19] I, Paul, am writing this with my own hand. I will pay it back – not to mention that you owe me your very self. [20] I do wish, brother, that I may have some benefit from you in the Lord; refresh my heart in Christ. [21] Confident of your obedience, I write to you, knowing that you will do even more than I ask.

"Welcome" (NIV, NRSV), "receive" (KJV) is *proslambanō*, literally, "take besides, take in addition." The connotation of the word here is "to extend a welcome, receive in(to) one's home or circle of acquaintances."[11] We see this usage several times in the New Testament (Romans 14:1, 3; 15:7; Acts 28:2) as a synonym of *dechomai*, "welcome," which we saw in Colossians 4:10 regarding John Mark. If Onesimus was indeed an escaped slave, Philemon had the legal right as a slave owner to punish Onesimus physically with a severe lashing – even if it ended in death. Slaves had no legal rights under Roman law. If he didn't want Onesimus in his household service any longer he could sell him, be rid of him, and regain some of his losses. But Paul appeals to him to "welcome him as you would welcome me" (verse 17b).

Moreover, Paul vouches for Onesimus to the extent that he offers to pay Philemon for any debt that Onesimus might have occurred, either through loss of labor or for anything he might have stolen to finance his escape. The verb is *apotinō*, a technical term that means, "make compensation, pay damages"[12]

Paul adds in verse 20a, "I do wish, brother, that I may have some benefit (*oninēmi*) from you in the Lord." "Benefit" (NIV, NRSV), "joy" is *oninēmi*, a play on words with

---

[11] *Proslambanō*, BDAG 883, 4.
[12] *Apotinō*, BDAG 124.

the name Onesimus. He is asking Philemon to ease his heart[13] with regard to his concern for Onesimus's future, to "refresh[14] my heart" (verse 20b).

Finally, Paul speaks of his assurance of Philemon's obedience (*hypakoē*). The word means, "state of being in compliance, obedience" (one listens and follows instructions).[15] Paul hasn't commanded Philemon, but he fully anticipates that Philemon will comply with his appeal.

A Gospel Partner (verse 17)

Notice how Paul begins his appeal: "So if you consider me a partner..." (verse 17). The word is *koinōnos*, "one who takes part in something with someone, companion, partner, sharer"[16] (closely related to the word *koinōnia*, "communion, sharing"). What does it mean to be a partner with Paul? It means that you share the same values, the same mission, and probably, that you have helped him financially in his work. As a partner, you take risks to achieve the mission, as well as receive in its rewards when the project bears fruit. The Philippian church, because of their financial contributions, had become partners or sharers in Paul's work (Philippians 1:5). To what degree are you a partner in the gospel? To what degree as a partner will you receive its rewards?

Prepare a Guest Room (verse 22)

Paul is now concluding his letter.

> "And one thing more: Prepare a guest room[17] for me, because I hope to be restored to you in answer to your prayers." (verse 22)

It would be common in a letter to mention the hope of visiting soon. However, his phrase, "and one thing more...." suggests that this sentence is actually part of his appeal. Paul's hopeful visit is in itself an inducement for Philemon to welcome Onesimus back.

Paul is serious, however. He is expecting to be released from confinement in Rome, "restored" (NIV, NRSV) or "given" (KJV). The word is *charizomai*, "give graciously... give or grant someone something,"[18] here, in answer to prayer.

---

[13] "Refresh my bowels" (KJV) may seem a bit crude, until you understand that "bowels" (*splanchnon*) is used to refer to ones inner feelings, one's "heart" (BDAG 938, 2).

[14] "Refresh" is *anapauō*, "to cause someone to gain relief from toil," here "cause to rest, give someone rest, refresh, revive" (BDAG 69, 1).

[15] *Hypakoē*, BDAG 1028, 1b.

[16] *Koinōnos*, BDAG 553, 1d.

[17] *Xenia*, "hospitality, entertainment" shown a guest, less frequently the place where the guest is lodged, "guest room" (BDAG 683).

Personal Greetings (verses 23-24)

"23 Epaphras, my fellow prisoner in Christ Jesus, sends you greetings. 24 And so do Mark, Aristarchus, Demas and Luke, my fellow workers." (verses 23-24)

We've commented on each of these "fellow workers" in lesson 8 above (Colossians 4:10, 12, 14). The Letter to Philemon seems to have been written at the same time as Colossians.

What Happened to Onesimus?

What happened as result of Paul's appeal for Onesimus? Did Philemon welcome him? Did he free him? Did he receive him as a Christian brother? Did he forgive him his theft and the loss of service?

We don't know the details from Scripture. But I would guess that the very existence of this short Letter to Philemon in the canon of scripture tells us that Philemon did indeed welcome Onesimus.

We do know than a man named Onesimus was bishop of Ephesus in the early second century, some 40 to 50 years later.[19] If Onesimus was but a young man in his latter teens or early twenties when Paul wrote the letter, it is possible that could have been a bishop at age 70. Perhaps this is the same Onesimus, the "unprofitable" slave whom Paul led to Christ and Philemon pardoned.[20]

What Do We Learn from this Letter?

Why is Philemon included among Paul's authentic letters, preserved for us down to this day? What are we to learn from it? Though it is not a didactic or teaching letter, there are several lessons found within it by implication:

---

[18] *Charizomai*, BDAG 1078, 1. We get our word "charismatic" or "gifted" from this word.

[19] Ignatius of Antioch (c. 110 AD), *Letter to the Ephesians* 1. In the *Constitutions of the Holy Apostles* (fourth century), Onesimus is mentioned as a freed slave in sec. 82 and bishop of Berea in Macedonia in sec. 46.

[20] Onesimus was a common name, especially of slaves. Several traditions exist that have been conflated with the Biblical Onesimus. Eastern Orthodox tradition venerates St. Onesimus. The questionable *History of the 70 Apostles* by Dorotheus, Bishop of Tyre states that Onesimus died in Potiole at the hands of the Roman ruler Tertillus. Another account (without attribution) indicates: "In the year 109, St. Onesimus was arrested and brought to trial before the Eparch Tertillus, during the reign of the Emperor Trajan. He held the saint in prison for eighteen days, and then sent him to prison in the city of Puteoli. After a while, the eparch sent for St Onesimus and had him stoned and beheaded for still maintaining his faith in Christ. A certain illustrious woman took the body of the martyr and placed it in a silver coffin." Another tradition sees Onesimus as Bishop of Byzantium 54 to 68 AD. See Lightfoot, *Colossians and Philemon*, p. 316.

1. We are not to command our equals to do the right thing. Paul appeals to Philemon to welcome Onesimus, but does not command him. In fact, he bends over backwards not to command him, even though he has the right (verses 8-9). With our children, it is appropriate to require right action. But with a grownup, we should appeal to their sense of right and wrong. People must make their own moral decisions.

2. Recompense is appropriate when we do wrong. Paul could not remove Onesimus's obligation to return to his master. He could appeal on his behalf. But Onesimus, even after his conversion and forgiveness by God, needed to do right by his master. This is found in steps 8 and 9 of the 12-Step Program of Alcoholics Anonymous:

> #8. Made a list of all persons we had harmed, and became willing to make amends to them all.

> #9. Made direct amends to such people wherever possible, except when to do so would injure them or others.

3. Sinners can change. Sometimes we do terrible things. But through God's grace we can change. Onesimus probably stole and ran away from his master. And, even though we believe slavery to be fundamentally wrong, in Paul's day, arbitrarily breaking that bond of slavery illegally was considered wrong. But in spite of Onesimus's sins, God got hold of him – in faraway Rome. And God changed him.

4. Christ changes relationships. Though people have different stations in life, Christ alters these relationships forever. As Paul wrote in Colossians:

> "Here there is no Greek or Jew, circumcised or uncircumcised, barbarian, Scythian, slave or free, but Christ is all, and is in all." (Colossians 3:11)

Even though Onesimus might be a slave in this life, now he is a brother in Christ. We are not to look down on people because of their social standing. To do so is a sin. We are all equal before God – and in Christ we are one!

5. We owe a debt to our spiritual fathers and mothers. When we become Christians, we now have a new kind of family. We have fathers and mothers in the Lord, and we owe them. In the case of our letter, Philemon was lost until Paul introduced him personally to Jesus Christ. As a result, Paul has a call on him: "Not to mention that you owe me your very self" (verse 19b).

6. Vouching for a brother or sister is a way of helping them to a new life. Vouching for someone is dangerous. We're advised in Proverbs not to be "surety" or "put up security" for either friends or strangers (Proverbs 6:1; 11:15). It's a bad business practice, because people, even friends, often disappoint us. But here we see Paul risking at least his capital of "good will" to help open up a new life for his friend and son in the Lord, Onesimus. We must be careful when we vouch for others. But sometimes it is the way that God can use us to bring reconciliation and restoration to those who don't deserve it. Christ vouches for us before God's throne, and has given every shred of his wealth to redeem us (1 John 2:1)!

Martin Luther liked this short book. "This epistle," he wrote, "shows a right noble lovely example of Christian love.... Even as Christ did for us with God the Father, thus also does St. Paul for Onesimus with Philemon... We are all his Onesimi, to my thinking."[21]

Q3. (Philemon 18-19) Paul vouches for Onesimus and puts up his money (at least in theory) to cover Onesimus's debts to Philemon? Is this wise in all cases? Why does Paul do it here? How does Christ vouch for us? When should we vouch for our Christian brothers and sisters?

http:/www.joyfulheart.com/forums/index.php?showtopic=991

Grace (verse 25)

"The grace of the Lord Jesus Christ be with your spirit." (verse 25)

A "grace wish" was a common way to end a letter in the Greek culture. But when Paul qualifies it with "the grace of the Lord Jesus Christ," he elevates grace to an entirely new level. He speaks of the grace of Jesus in his official title and in all his glory. He is speaking of the unmerited favor of God poured out to us through the suffering, death, and resurrection of Jesus Christ.

Dear friends, Philemon needed God's grace to cope with the emotions that crowded up in him as he considered his runaway slave Onesimus, now before him. And we need grace too, as we consider where we came from, what we are facing, and where we are going. Thank God for grace!

Paul's final greeting is a fitting way to conclude these lessons on Colossians and Philemon: "May the grace of the Lord Jesus Christ be with your spirit!" Amen.

---

[21] Cited by Lightfoot, *Colossians and Philemon*, pp. 317-318.

Prayer

Father, thank you for the times you've helped us to forgive and move on when our hearts have been clouded with hurt and anger. Thank you for the grace you gave Philemon to make the decision that he must make. Help us, too. In Jesus' name, we pray. Amen.

Appendix 1. Participant Handouts

If you're working with a class or small group, feel free to duplicate the following handouts in this appendix at no additional charge. If you'd like to print 8-1/2" x 11" sheets, you can download the free Participant Guide handout sheets at: **www.jesuswalk.com/colossians/colossians-lesson-handouts.pdf**

Discussion Questions

You'll find 4 to 5 questions for each lesson. Each question may include several sub-questions. These are designed to get group members engaged in discussion of the key points of the passage. If you're running short of time, feel free to skip questions or portions of questions.

Lessons

Introduction

1. A Prayer for the Colossian Believers (1:1-14)

2. The Supremacy of Christ (1:15-19)

3. Christ the Reconciler (1:20-23)

4. Paul's Labors for the Church (1:24-2:5)

5. Freedom from Legalism (2:6-23)

6. Guidelines for Holy Living (3:1-17)

7. Christian Households (3:18-4:1)

8. Final Instructions and Greetings (4:2-18)

9. Paul's Letter to Philemon

Introduction to Paul's Letter to the Colossians

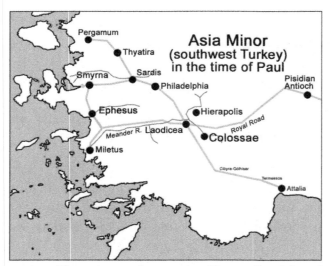

City of Colossae

Colossae is an ancient city located about 100 miles east of Ephesus in present-day southwest Turkey. It was a smaller city, about 10-15 miles from its larger cousins in the Lycus River Valley – Laodicea and Hierapolis. It was near the Royal Road that ran from Ephesus east all the way to Persia.

Peoples

The population was a mixture of native Phrygians plus a significant Jewish minority who were settled in the region centuries before.

History of the Church

The church had been founded by Epaphras, who had probably heard the gospel when Paul had been teaching for nearly three years in Ephesus, 53-55 AD.

Authorship and Date

The letter was written by the Apostle Paul while in prison, probably in Rome approximately 60-62 AD (Acts 20:31-32).

Occasion of the Letter

The church is only a few years old and being threatened by an unsettling heresy. Epaphras makes his way to Rome, finds Paul in prison, and asks him to write an apostolic letter to the church that will strengthen them in their faith.

Nature of the "Colossian Heresy"

Though the exact identity of the false teachers is debated by scholars, this seems to be an ascetic and mystical variety of Judaism, perhaps with a Christian twist.

Paul seems to characterize it (as you read between the lines in Colossians 2:8-25) as a philosophy that promoted, among other things: food restrictions and Jewish holy days, ascetic disciplines, angel worship, visionary experiences, and rule-keeping. In all this, tradition was central, rather than Christ. The believers were in danger of becoming in bondage to man-made traditions, rather than free in Christ.

The false teachers acted as if their religious practice was superior to the believers'.

Purpose of the Letter

1. To encourage and ground this relatively new Christian community, and

2. To protect them from the seduction of false teachers, probably from a variety of mystical Judaism, that tended to denigrate these Gentile Christians' faith in Christ in favor of the claims of Judaism.

1. A Prayer for the Colossian Believers (Colossians 1:1-14)

Discussion Questions

Q1. (Colossians 1:5-6) Paul glorifies the gospel, the good news. What words does he use to describe the action of the gospel in verses 5 and 6? Given the temptation the recipients have to adopt another religious philosophy, why do you think he reminds them of the world scope of the gospel's influence? What happens in our day when a church becomes embarrassed or unimpressed with the gospel message? How does this affect the church?

Q2. (Colossians 1:9-12a) What are the elements of Paul's prayer for the Colossian believers? What are the seven or eight specific results that he prays will be produced in their lives? Which of these are most important in a Christian disciple? Which, do you think, are least important? What happens when some are missing?

Q3. (Colossians 1:12-13) Why does Paul use the terms darkness and light to portray his readers past and future? Why does he remind them where they came from? What is "the inheritance of the saints in light" that he mentions? In verse 13 we find two terms used of governing bodies? How are they contrasted in verse 13? In what sense are subjects "governed" in each?

Q4. (Colossians 1:12-13) What are the three or four action verbs in verses 12 and 13 that paint a picture of salvation? Who performs the action? Who is it performed on? In what way were we "qualified/enabled/made meet"? In what way were we "rescued" or "delivered"?

Q5. (Colossians 1:13-14) What are the two qualities mentioned in verse 14 that characterize the "kingdom of his beloved Son"? What did the idea of redemption mean in the Greek? In what way did Christ "redeem" us? What is the significance of the fact that our sins are forgiven in this kingdom?

Key Verses

"All over the world this gospel is bearing fruit and growing, just as it has been doing among you since the day you heard it and understood God's grace in all its truth." (Colossians 1:6, NIV)

"For he has rescued us from the dominion of darkness and brought us into the kingdom of the Son he loves, in whom we have redemption, the forgiveness of sins." (Colossians 1:13-14, NIV)

2. The Supremacy of Christ (Colossians 1:15-1:23)

Discussion Questions

Q1. (Colossians 1:15a, 19) The great understanding of Judaism was that God is spirit, not physical. That he is invisible. Any idol that tries to depict him is blasphemous. So what is the significance of the statement that Jesus is "the image of the invisible God"? According to verse 19, to what degree does this image accurately represent God? Is Jesus actually God in the flesh, or only a manifestation of God, a kind of holograph?*

*A holograph might be like Princess Leia in Star Wars sending a message through R2-D2: "Help me Obi-Wan Kenobi, you're my only hope...."

Q2. (Colossians 1:15b-17) What does "firstborn of all creation/every creature" mean? Is Jesus a created being? If not, what does "firstborn" mean here? What do verses 16-17 teach about Jesus' pre-existence? What does verse 16b teach about the purpose of creation? According to verse 17, what is Jesus' past role in creation? What is his present role in creation?

Q3. (Colossians 1:16) "Thrones," "powers," "rulers," "principalities," "authorities," etc. probably refer to both earthly as well as angelic and demonic dominions. What does this passage teach about the relation of these powers to Jesus? How should this affect our fear of them? How should it affect our prayers?

Q4. (Colossians 1:18) How should the assertion that Jesus is the "head of the body, the church" affect the way we conceive of the church? Is he talking about the universal church or a local congregation, or both? If we believe that Jesus is the head of the church, how should that affect the way we "do church"? In what ways does the visible church represent the "head"? How well do we do it?

Key Verse

"For by him all things were created: things in heaven and on earth, visible and invisible, whether thrones or powers or rulers or authorities; all things were created by him and for him. He is before all things, and in him all things hold together." (Colossians 1:16-17, NIV)

3. Christ the Reconciler (Colossians 1:20-23)

Discussion Questions

Q1. (Colossians 1:20-22). What does "reconcile" mean? What was our state before reconciliation? (verse 21)

Q2. (Colossians 1:20-22) By what means did Jesus accomplish this reconciliation? What does "the blood of his cross" have to do with it? What is the purpose of this reconciliation (verse 22)? To whom are we "presented" (verse 22)?

Q3. (Colossians 1:22) How can we be presented "holy," "without blemish," and "free from accusation" since we are not perfect? How is this possible?

Q4. (Colossians 1:23) If our salvation depends upon the grace of God, not us, why is it necessary for us to "continue in your faith, established and firm, not moved"? What happens if we don't? What is the nature of the security we have in Jesus according to this text (and this text only*)?

*Please don't use proof texts from other verses in the New Testament, but interpret Colossians 1:23 in its appropriate context.

Key Verse

"But now he has reconciled you by Christ's physical body through death to present you holy in his sight, without blemish and free from accusation-- if you continue in your faith, established and firm, not moved from the hope held out in the gospel." (Colossians 1:22-23a, NIV)

4. Paul's Labors for the Church (Colossians 1:24-2:5)

Discussion Questions

Q1. (Colossians 1:24) How could Paul's sufferings in prison complete what is lacking in Christ's afflictions? Is Paul referring to Christ's sufferings on the cross? Or is he seeing suffering in some kind of cosmic sense? If so, in what sense are your sufferings for Christ of value to the church?

Q2. (Colossians 1:26-27) What is the mystery that Paul talks about? In what sense was, "Christ in you, the hope of glory," hidden prior to this? In what sense is "glory" used here? What does "the hope of glory" mean in this context?

Q3. (Colossians 1:28-2:1) What is the purpose of Paul's labors according to verse 28? What does "perfect in Christ" mean? How does Paul accomplish this goal? In what way is he "struggling" for them?

Q4. (Colossians 2:2-3) In what sense are "all the treasures of wisdom and knowledge" hidden in Christ? What does that mean?

Key Verses

"To them God has chosen to make known among the Gentiles the glorious riches of this mystery, which is Christ in you, the hope of glory." (Colossians 1:27, NIV)

"We proclaim him, admonishing and teaching everyone with all wisdom, so that we may present everyone perfect in Christ." (Colossians 1:28, NIV)

"... Christ, in whom are hidden all the treasures of wisdom and knowledge." (Colossians 2:2b-3, NIV)

5. Freedom from Legalism (Colossians 2:6-23)

Discussion Questions

Q1. (Colossians 2:8) Philosophy refers to a prevailing belief system. How can a belief system be empty and false? Have you ever personally experienced being captivated by a belief system only to find it deceptive and hollow?

Q2. (Colossians 2:9-10) What does verse 9 teach about Christ's full divinity? In what sense are we "complete" or "come to fullness" in Christ? What does this mean? Why do we sometimes fail to understand this fullness?

Q3. (Colossians 2:13-15) How did forgiveness free us from the Law? What is the significance of nailing the Law to the cross? What does this symbolize? How did the cross bring triumph over evil spiritual forces?

Q4. (Colossians 2:20-23) Why are legalism and asceticism unable to restrain the sinful nature? What alternative to legalism does Paul offer in Colossians 2?

Key Verses

"God made you alive with Christ. He forgave us all our sins, having canceled the written code, with its regulations, that was against us and that stood opposed to us; he took it away, nailing it to the cross." (Colossians 2:13b-14, NIV)

"And having disarmed the powers and authorities, he made a public spectacle of them, triumphing over them by the cross." (Colossians 2:15, NIV)

"These are a shadow of the things that were to come; the reality, however, is found in Christ." (Colossians 2:17, NIV)

6. Guidelines for Holy Living (Colossians 3:1-17)

Discussion Questions

Q1. (Colossians 3:1-2) What does it mean to "set your heart/mind" on the things above? Does this mean that we're "too heavenly minded to be of any earthly good"? If not, what *does* it mean? What happens when we don't take control and direct our thinking and meditating?

Q2. (Colossians 3:5) Why is sexual lust so difficult for people, especially males? Though we cannot deny that we are sexual beings, how can we keep sexual desire from controlling us and causing us to sin?

Q3. (Colossians 3:8) Why are sins of the tongue so easy to slip into? In what ways do they damage us and others? How can we break free of sins of the tongue?

Q4. (Colossians 3:12-14) Why are Christian virtues so important to Christ? Why are they so important to the church? Why are they so important to non-Christians? Why are they so important in our homes?

Key Verses

"Set your minds on things above, not on earthly things. For you died, and your life is now hidden with Christ in God." (Colossians 3:2-3, NIV)

"Bear with each other and forgive whatever grievances you may have against one another. Forgive as the Lord forgave you." (Colossians 3:13, NIV)

"And whatever you do, whether in word or deed, do it all in the name of the Lord Jesus, giving thanks to God the Father through him." (Colossians 3:17, NIV)

7. Christian Households (Colossians 3:18-4:1)

Discussion Questions

Q1. (Colossians 3:18-19) Why do you think Paul chose these directions to give to wives and husbands – considering all the things he could have said? Why is true submission difficult for wives? Why is unselfish love difficult for husbands? What prompts harshness in a husband? Is the cause inner or outer?

Q2. (Colossians 3:20-21) In what way does obedience prepare a child for everyday life in the future? For spiritual life in the future? What can fathers do to keep from discouraging their children?

Q3. (Colossians 3:22-24) If you apply Paul's instructions to slaves to the role of being an employee, what is the role of sincerity as an employee? How do we live this out when working under a poor boss? In what sense are we actually "working for the Lord"? What would happen in the workplace, if we actually began to live by these attitudes of heart?

Q4. (Colossians 3:25-4:1) What instructions does Paul give masters – or employers, in our culture? What would happen in the workplace if employers sought to live by this rule?

Key Verse

Whatever you do, work at it with all your heart, as working for the Lord, not for men, since you know that you will receive an inheritance from the Lord as a reward. It is the Lord Christ you are serving. (Colossians 3:23-24, NIV)

8. Final Instructions and Greetings (Colossians 4:2-18)

Discussion Questions

Q1. (Colossians 4:2) What guidelines does Paul give us to form our praying habits? If you put these into practice fully, how would they affect your prayer life? What problems would they help correct?

Q2. (Colossians 4:3-4) What prayer request does Paul ask of the Colossian believers? What does it mean to pray for an "open door." Why does he ask for prayer in communicating the gospel? Isn't he an "old hand" at this? Why does he need help?

Q3. (Colossians 4:5-6) What instructions does Paul give us in sharing our faith with non-believers? Why, do you think, we sometimes let opportunities slip by? How will our conversation being "full of grace" help us represent Christ well?

Q4. (Colossians 4:17) Why do you think Archippus was singled out in verse 17? If you could invent a story of his role in the Colossian church, how would you describe Archippus? In what ways does he remind you of yourself?

Key Verses

"Devote yourselves to prayer, being watchful and thankful." (Colossians 4:2, NIV)

"Be wise in the way you act toward outsiders; make the most of every opportunity. Let your conversation be always full of grace, seasoned with salt, so that you may know how to answer everyone." (Colossians 4:5-6, NIV)

"Tell Archippus: 'See to it that you complete the work you have received in the Lord.'" (Colossians 4:17, NIV)

9. Paul's Letter to Philemon

Discussion Questions

Q1. (Philemon 12) Why does Paul send Onesimus back to Philemon where he can lose his freedom again? Why is it necessary for Paul to do this? Why is it necessary for Onesimus to do this?

Q2. (Philemon 14) Why doesn't Paul come right out and command Philemon? Is this out of respect for his personhood or to build moral character in him -- or what?

Q3. (Philemon 18-19) Paul vouches for Onesimus and puts up his money (at least in theory) to cover Onesimus's debts to Philemon? Is this wise in all cases? Why does Paul do it here? How does Christ vouch for us? When should we vouch for our Christian brothers and sisters?

Appendix 2. Songs and Hymns from Colossians

While there are many, many songs based on themes from the companion book of Ephesians, Colossians has apparently inspired only a few hymns, choruses, and praise songs. Here are some that I found:

1:5-20   **"Light of the World,"** by Matt Redman (©1999, Thankyou Music)

1:10   **"Walk Worthy,"** by J. Paul Williams and Joseph M. Martin (© 1995, Timespann Music, Inc.)

1:15-18   **"God of the Ages,"** by Travis Doucette (© 2008, Music You Can't Turn Down)

1:15-18   **"Jesus Alone,"** by Brian Doerksen and Craig Musseau (©1992, Vineyard Songs Canada, ION Publishing)

1:20   **"Glory to His Name"** (or "Down at the Cross"), by Elisha Albright Hoffman and John Hart Stockton

1:27   **"Rejoice"** ("Christ is in you/the hope of glory in our hearts"), by Graham Kendrick (©1983, Thankyou Music)

1:27   **"Everything,"** by Tim Hughes (©2005, Thankyou Music)

2:9-10   **"Complete in Him,"** by Tom Fettke (©1977, Pilot Point Music)

3:1   **"If Ye Then Be Risen with Christ,"** by Linda Michieli (©1971 Doulos Publishing)

3:1   **"Turn Your Eyes upon Jesus,"** words and music by Helen H. Lemmel (1922)

3:1-3, 15   **"On Things Above (Colossians 3),"** by Jimmie Young (©2005 Mass Voice Music)

3:13   **"Forgive,"** by Jay Stocker (©2006, Group Publishing, Inc.)

3:14   **"We Are One in the Bond of Love,"** by Otis Skillings (©1971 Lillenas Publishing Company)

3:15-17   **"Wedding Song from Colossians,"** by Richard Proulx (©1993, G.I.A. Publications)

3:17   **"Whatever You Do,"** by Jay Stocker (©2006, Group Publishing, Inc.)

3:17   **"In Everything Give Thanks,"** by Gary Sadler (©1993 Integrity's Hosanna!
            Music)

3:23   **"Colossians 3:23,"** by Colin Buchanan (2008, Wanaaring Road Music)

4:2   **"Let Us Pray,"** by Stephen Curtis Chapman (©1996, Sparrow Song, Peach
            Hill Songs)

CPSIA information can be obtained
at www.ICGtesting.com
Printed in the USA
BVOW09s2239070517

483459BV00009B/194/P